NATIONAL DEFENSE RESEARCH INSTITUTE

T0303344

Developing an Assessment, Monitoring, and Evaluation Framework for U.S. Department of Defense Security Cooperation

Jefferson P. Marquis, Michael J. McNerney, S. Rebecca Zimmerman, Merrie Archer, Jeremy Boback, David Stebbins

Prepared for the Office of the Secretary of Defense

For more information on this publication, visit www.rand.org/t/RR1611

Library of Congress Cataloging-in-Publication Data is available for this publication.
ISBN: 978-0-8330-9670-8

Published by the RAND Corporation, Santa Monica, Calif.
© Copyright 2016 RAND Corporation
RAND® is a registered trademark.

Cover: U.S. Marine Corps photo by Cpl. Brittany J. Kohler/Released.

Support RAND
Make a tax-deductible charitable contribution at
www.rand.org/giving/contribute

www.rand.org

Preface

At a time when the United States is increasingly relying on foreign partners for its security and attempting to build their military capacity, security cooperation activities and expenditures can no longer be justified with anecdotal evidence. In order to gauge security cooperation's "return on investment," senior leaders in the presidential administration and Congress are requesting a rigorous accounting of what is being done, what is being spent, and what is being achieved and not being achieved in relation to specific planning objectives across the security cooperation enterprise. Although many parts of the U.S. Department of Defense (DoD) already conduct some form of security cooperation–related assessments, monitoring, and/or evaluation, understanding and implementation vary widely. Without high-level DoD leadership, these efforts will likely remain ad hoc and difficult to regularize and aggregate in a manner useful for planning and management at various levels of DoD or for coordination and collaboration with security assistance sector partners outside the department.

This report seeks to address the challenge of creating a DoD-wide system for security cooperation assessment, monitoring, and evaluation (AME): first, by analyzing existing planning and AME processes and practices inside and outside DoD to understand what works and what does not in different contexts; and second, by presenting a conceptual framework that explains how AME methods might be applied, integrated, and implemented by major security cooperation organizations so that they conform as closely as possible to analytic best practices and existing DoD policies, plans, and processes. To execute this approach, the study team analyzed documents, interviewed subject-matter experts within and outside DoD, and sponsored a workshop with security cooperation officials in the Washington, D.C., region.

This report should be valuable for defense and foreign policy analysts with an interest in security cooperation.

This research was sponsored by the Deputy Assistant Secretary of Defense for Security Cooperation and conducted within the International Security and Defense Policy Center of the RAND National Defense Research Institute, a federally funded research and development center sponsored by the Office of the Secretary of Defense, the Joint Staff, the Unified Combatant Commands, the Navy, the Marine Corps, the defense agencies, and the defense Intelligence Community.

For more information on the RAND International Security and Defense Policy Center, see www.rand.org/nsrd/ndri/centers/isdp or contact the director (contact information is provided on the web page).

Contents

Figures and Tables

Figures

Tables

Summary

Every year, the U.S. Department of Defense (DoD) conducts thousands of cooperative activities with officials from security institutions and with security forces around the world. How effective are these activities? Answering this question is challenging, to say the least. Yet, given the priority placed on security cooperation in U.S. government strategies and the billions of dollars spent on its execution, the answer goes to the heart of understanding the success or failure of U.S. foreign policy.

How can senior policymakers, members of Congress, and the American people better understand security cooperation? Why is DoD working with particular foreign countries, and in what ways? How is security cooperation expected to make a difference? How does DoD monitor these activities to ensure that everything is on track? Most importantly, what is working, and what is not? The answers to these questions are sometimes very specific, but more often they are broad and unclear, especially for those far from the action.

Understanding security cooperation starts with understanding its objectives. As a precursor to this report, RAND researchers conducted a study to help DoD develop specific, measurable, achievable, relevant and results-oriented, and time-bound (SMART) security cooperation objectives.[1] Not every objective can meet every one of these criteria on its own; some must be supplemented with information about the tasks

---

[1]   Michael J. McNerney, Jefferson P. Marquis, S. Rebecca Zimmerman, and Ariel Klein, *SMART Security Cooperation Objectives: Improving DoD Planning and Guidance*, Santa Monica, Calif.: RAND Corporation, RR-1430-OSD, 2016.

planned within each objective. When detailed objectives and tasks are combined with an assessment, monitoring, and evaluation (AME) regime, an organization can create a system in which the whole will be greater than the sum of its parts.

In the AME construct, *assessment* means that senior leaders must have a baseline assessment. What is the security environment in which these activities will take place? What are the partner's existing capabilities, and what does the United States want to improve? How well-aligned are the partner's interests and values with those of the United States? *Monitoring* means that priority efforts must be closely tracked to determine whether inputs (e.g., money and effort) are translating into outputs (e.g., equipment, training, education, and information). These outputs then serve as the basis for tracking progress toward objectives (i.e., outcomes). *Evaluation* examines outcomes and is crucial to understanding what is working and what is not. Success is not ultimately measured by the provision of equipment or training; it is measured by the extent to which security cooperation activities help achieve U.S. objectives. Investments require following up to make sure that they yield the full potential benefits that were expected. Many organizations inside and outside the U.S. government have put a heavy emphasis on the ability to evaluate progress toward objectives, but translating their ever-evolving best practices into an AME framework that can be applied to an organization as large and complex as DoD presents quite a challenge.

RAND has provided analytic support to the Office of the Secretary of Defense (OSD) as it has worked to tackle this challenge over several years. For example, in 2009, RAND developed a framework for security cooperation assessments, with a focus on program-level analysis.[2] More recently, RAND analyzed many of the key concepts that form the foundation of a robust assessment program, including

---

[2]   Jennifer D. P. Moroney, Jefferson P. Marquis, Cathryn Quantic Thurston, and Gregory F. Treverton, *A Framework to Assess Programs for Building Partnerships*, Santa Monica, Calif.: RAND Corporation, MG-863-OSD, 2009.

logic models, inputs, outputs, and outcomes.[3] As we discuss later in this report, these studies and other research have helped many components in DoD to develop various aspects of AME systems. OSD asked RAND to build on its existing research and the ongoing efforts of practitioners to help it create a comprehensive, DoD-wide AME regime informed by the best methods in current theory and practice.

RAND's approach to this request had two principal components: (1) an analysis of existing planning and AME processes and practices inside and outside DoD to understand what works and what does not in different contexts and (2) the development of a conceptual framework that explains how AME methods might be applied, integrated, and implemented by major security cooperation organizations so that they conform as closely as possible to analytic best practices and existing DoD policies, plans, and processes. To execute this approach, the team analyzed documents, interviewed subject-matter experts within and outside DoD, and sponsored a workshop with security cooperation officials in the Washington, D.C., region.

Combatant Command Planning and AME

Because so much of the planning for security cooperation activities occurs at DoD's combatant commands (CCMDs), the research team started by analyzing CCMD guidance, planning processes, and existing AME efforts, particularly those at U.S. European Command (EUCOM) and U.S. Pacific Command (PACOM). We found that both commands have extensive and increasingly sophisticated systems in place for AME. They have staff dedicated to AME (for which they use "assessments" as a blanket term). They have designed their planning processes to analyze the security capabilities of partner nations, monitor progress, and review the results of past activities. These systems, however, are far from comprehensive, vary widely across CCMDs, tend

---

[3]   Christopher Paul, Brian J. Gordon, Jennifer D. P. Moroney, Lisa Saum-Manning, Beth Grill, Colin P. Clarke, and Heather Peterson, *A Building Partner Capacity Assessment Framework: Tracking Inputs, Outputs, Outcomes, Disrupters, and Workarounds*, Santa Monica, Calif.: RAND Corporation, RR-935-OSD, 2015.

to focus on meeting the information needs of the command itself, and emphasize functional and mission objectives (using lines of effort and lines of activity) over objectives that focus on the partner country as a whole or a particular program as a whole. Country and program objectives are of great interest to senior Department of State and DoD leaders, as well as Congress, but they often struggle to translate CCMD AME results into information that can help them make decisions or provide oversight.

As described in Chapter Five, we recommend several steps to improve CCMD AME, including the following:

- OSD should update planning guidance to direct the development of AME reporting in support of civilian oversight requirements, while allowing CCMDs and services to tailor some aspects of reporting for their own needs. The details for this reporting—including templates like those discussed in Chapters Three and Four—could be provided in the AME handbook recommended in the next section.
- Because best practices are not static, OSD should incorporate continuous learning concepts into security cooperation planning guidance.
- OSD should adjust DoD security cooperation guidance and leverage planning and programming reviews to increase senior DoD leader focus on getting useful reporting from CCMDs.
- OSD should sponsor a workshop session with a wide range of stakeholders on how DoD can better incorporate program- and country-focused AME into security cooperation planning and reporting. CCMD staff could discuss how they incorporate AME into their theater campaign plans, while other stakeholders could discuss what data and analytic support they require to assess, monitor, and evaluate security cooperation. In addition to better leveraging theater campaign plans, the workshop could consider the other reporting requirements discussed in Chapter Four.

Relevant AME Frameworks

Understanding program efficacy is central to how organizations learn and improve their performance. In developing our DoD-wide AME framework, we reviewed case studies representing several other relevant AME systems. The study team analyzed cases from the U.S. Army and U.S. Air Force, select DoD security cooperation programs, the Organisation for Economic Co-operation and Development (OECD), the U.S. Agency for International Development (USAID), the Department of State, the Millennium Challenge Corporation (MCC), and the World Bank Group (WBG).

DoD

The Army and Air Force have each developed frameworks for partner country capability and interoperability assessments. If fully implemented, their efforts could provide useful information to security cooperation planners and programmers who lack relevant expertise or service perspectives on what is needed from partner militaries. Neither service, however, has established a systematic process for injecting its partner country assessments into joint and interagency planning and programming to, thereby, break out of the intra-service "bubble."

In terms of particular security cooperation programs, OSD has developed a useful AME process for the Section 1206/2282 program, which provides training and equipment for counterterrorism and other missions. The program is founded on a logic model that describes how planned investments (inputs) will translate into detailed results (outputs and outcomes). It is noteworthy for its use of a team of independent evaluators and its five categories for assessing partner capabilities and progress. It is exemplary for its procedural clarity, particularly its use of a handbook that describes the system in detail.

The study team also analyzed DoD programs focused on developing partner country defense institutions (defense institution-building [DIB]). While many of these programs were in the early stages of developing AME systems at the time of our research (spring 2015 to spring 2016), a few challenges and best practices emerged from our analysis. Implementing AME for the diverse array of DIB programs

xiv   Developing an AME Framework for DoD Security Cooperation

highlighted the challenges inherent in establishing any DoD-wide AME framework for security cooperation. Because DIB programs generally are long term and implemented by U.S.-based personnel, rather than regionally based personnel, AME standardization and data collection are difficult. However, AME can likely be further standardized through a common logic model and mission set, as with Section 1206/2282 programs. The use by OSD's Ministry of Defense Advisors program of needs assessments, execution plans, and evaluation plans in its AME frameworks is a best practice that could be applied to other DIB programs and beyond.

In Chapter Five, we describe several recommendations that are based on our analysis of these AME frameworks, including the following:

- OSD should incorporate service best practices in partner assessments into future security cooperation AME guidance.
- Joint Staff should work with service security cooperation planners to develop an approach for injecting service partner country assessments into joint and interagency planning and programming.
- OSD should task the Defense Security Cooperation Agency (DSCA) to develop a handbook for program-level AME. This AME handbook could be modeled on the 1206/2282 handbook but could include additional materials drawn from the framework described in Chapter Four.
- OSD should work with DSCA to develop general theories of change and a set of logic models for common capability development areas, such as engagements, exercises, education, train and equip activities, and institution-building.
- OSD should include in the program-level AME handbook a section on DIB that incorporates best practices from the Ministry of Defense Advisors program and other DIB programs.

Beyond DoD

While OECD does not have an AME system for the international community to use, it does have a security sector reform handbook and a set of principles for evaluation. Security sector reform experts in the United States and internationally use OECD as a forum for discussing how to implement these principles and share best practices.

Most Department of State and USAID officials treat assessments as a program management function (as part of planning processes) and address them separately from monitoring and evaluations. USAID's Interagency Security Sector Assessment Framework (ISSAF), which the Department of State has used, is an exception and a potentially valuable model for DoD. The ISSAF provides a multistep process to identify capability and capacity shortfalls, barriers to change, and political will and to prioritize responses to these challenges.

Both the Department of State and USAID have robust monitoring and evaluation regimes through the use of the "Managing for Results" framework and highly trained evaluation teams. Whereas the Department of State's efforts—particularly in the security sector—are not fully integrated across programs, USAID promotes quality and unity of effort through common training and an evidence-based AME culture across the agency. Because the Department of State, like DoD, manages a vast array of programs, its programs lean on a set of standard indicators tied to a standardized program structure and a common reporting portal to better integrate its AME efforts. Standard indicators and a program structure provide a level of quasi-automation in the AME process that may make it vastly easier to collect and aggregate relevant data from all operating units. While DoD could benefit from standardization, any efforts in this area bring several challenges in such areas as training, incentives to provide inputs, and complementary tailored evaluations with plain language narratives and additional qualitative data. USAID offers a robust set of templates that guide program managers in designing evaluation scopes of work. This may be a transferrable practice.

One of the features that stands out when analyzing the MCC approach to AME is the extensive level of partner country involvement that stems from its compact model, which requires host nation partnership. The MCC and partner country must produce a monitoring and evaluation plan at the start of any program, which includes a data collection plan to support several categories of indicators. The partner writes a "constraints analysis," which seeks to identify root causes of lack of growth and is the document used to guide program design. Evaluations are conducted by independent teams, composed of competitively selected, trained evaluators.

While the WBG has confusing terminology around assessment and monitoring, it does take a rigorous approach to AME. For example, its Systematic Country Diagnostics function is a master, country-level assessment to guide both the country strategy and projects management. WBG dedicates 1.3 percent of program funding to AME. It uses decentralized self-evaluations reviewed by independent experts. This approach may help to resolve some of the burden of work that would otherwise fall on independent evaluators in the DoD context.

In Chapter Five, we describe several recommendations, based on our analysis of these non-DoD AME frameworks, including the following:

- OSD should engage with OECD security sector reform experts to discuss lessons from conducing AME in security sector environments and the refinement of its approach.
- OSD should build a very limited menu of standard monitoring indicators, as well as a means for tailoring particular indicators to account for context.
- Using examples from the Department of State, USAID, MCC, and WBG, OSD should develop templates for staff to use in designing their monitoring and evaluation approaches, which could help ensure consistent understanding of terminology, data requirements, analytic methods, and timelines. OSD should also solicit help from USAID staff in developing concrete steps to improve AME training within DoD.
- OSD should develop a personnel exchange between DoD and MCC staff to stimulate innovation.
- OSD should consider incorporating aspects of MCC's approach to producing a monitoring and evaluation plan developed jointly by the United States and partner nation at the start of any program to strengthen host nation participation and political will.

- OSD and DSCA should meet with World Bank and USAID AME experts to discuss the processes by which different organizations fund AME efforts.

DoD-Wide AME Framework

To meet administration and congressional requirements, as well as its own needs for greater accountability and improved decisionmaking, DoD needs to create a strategic framework that integrates its various initiatives in the security cooperation realm, including those related to AME, and takes advantage of relevant lessons learned from other security sector assistance organizations. Although many parts of DoD already conduct some form of assessments, monitoring, and/or evaluation, understanding and implementation vary widely. The framework in Chapter Four explains the fundamental elements of AME, establishes common definitions, and specifies a five-step approach for incorporating the framework into security cooperation planning, program design, and implementation.

The framework also describes various methods for DoD management of AME, ultimately recommending a hybrid approach to AME that is neither fully centralized nor decentralized. Because of DoD's size and the complexity of its missions, the framework recommends decentralized assessments and monitoring. Assessments may be best conducted and managed at the CCMD level, with monitoring at the implementation level. Evaluations, however, may be best performed at the policy and institutional levels, given the civilian oversight requirements for the Secretary of Defense and senior staff.

To stimulate the process of integrating AME into larger security cooperation processes, the framework includes a five-step cycle, which begins with an initial contextual assessment and collection of baseline data. This step is followed by the incorporation of AME results into planning (step two) and program design (step three). Step four focuses on monitoring the plan and implementing the program, and step five focuses on centralized evaluation. In our description of the AME cycle, we have chosen to use the country plan as our primary unit of analysis because it provides a holistic perspective of the desired outcomes and impact of security cooperation efforts. However, the methodology and standards that we describe for integrating AME into country planning are mostly adaptable to security cooperation programs and functional lines of effort as well.

In analyzing the roles and responsibilities for AME, it became clear that effective DoD-wide monitoring and evaluation of security cooperation requires a collective analysis of progress achieved against planning objectives, as defined by a small set of indicators. While each CCMD, military service, or other component may require its own tailored objectives and indicators, some should be standardized for strategic decisionmaking purposes. In addition to working from standardized objectives and indicators, it was clear from our research that AME implementation for a complex organization like DoD requires the use of several well-coordinated reporting documents and supporting tools.

After describing the basic hybrid AME management approach, how it is incorporated into planning, and general roles and responsibilities, the framework describes a more developed performance management system, based on our findings from analyzing other AME frameworks. The proposed system includes policy, planning, tracking, analytic, and reporting components, as well as a collaborative function that allows for stakeholder feedback on the AME system itself.

Finally, the framework provides an illustrative approach for the security cooperation performance management system to prioritize which countries, programs, and functions should undergo rigorous assessments and which should undergo rigorous evaluations. These potential prioritization methods are based on our analysis of other AME systems and are purposely simplified and generalized, with the understanding that a final approach will depend in large part on the final contours of DoD's framework and on additional stakeholder inputs.

In Chapter Five, we describe several recommendations, based on our development of this DoD-wide AME framework, including the following:

- OSD should expedite issuance of security cooperation AME policy guidance, including establishment of roles and responsibilities. Guidance should come in several types of documents, such as planning guidance, program guidance, formal memos, and informal handbooks and standard operating procedures. Guidance should be supplemented with socialization at security cooperation annual workshops and other fora. The framework in this report can serve as a useful starting point for developing the necessary guidance and processes, but, at a minimum, we recommend the following actions:
  - OSD should develop a DoD instruction for AME that would clarify AME policy, terminology, roles and responsibilities, and standards across the defense enterprise.
  - OSD should institute a requirement for a report for the Secretary of Defense and Congress to share results of priority country evaluations and program evaluations.
  - OSD should chair an AME working group to determine content, processes, and timing for AME inputs to the reporting requirements identified in our proposed AME framework in Chapter Four. The working group could also discuss how to better leverage existing tools like the Global Theater Security Cooperation Management Information System to support monitoring of activities and resources and their connection to SMART objectives—and how to develop a new tool for managing strategic level planning and evaluation.
- OSD should subject its AME guidance to frequent testing and revising, particularly in the first few years. Over the longer term, OSD should strive to achieve a greater level of AME standardization and methodological rigor across DoD. Such standardization should improve AME performance, allow DoD to evaluate progress over time, and improve collaboration with security sector assistance partners across the U.S. government and internationally.
- OSD should work with Joint Staff, DSCA, CCMDs, and other stakeholders to institute a hybrid performance management model with decentralized assessment and monitoring and central-

ized evaluation. As described in Chapter Four, this model would drive a system that delegates the bulk of AME data collection and analysis to CCMDs, military services, other DoD agencies, and the Intelligence Community, while maintaining OSD and Joint Staff oversight of evaluation efforts.

- OSD and DSCA should identify funding for a centralized, independent evaluation organization, as well as an organization to support and synchronize performance and effectiveness monitoring.
- OSD should lead an effort to develop a template with a small, focused set of standardized SMART objectives and performance/effectiveness indicators to be used as a model. CCMDs and other stakeholders would supplement these standardized objective and indicators with their own, tailored ones.
- The AME working group described above should develop a prioritization scheme, using the notional examples in Chapter Four as a starting point.

Conclusion

Security cooperation stakeholders at the CCMD, service, and program levels have made substantial progress assessing, monitoring, and evaluating security cooperation; and interest by senior policymakers, the requirements of the Presidential Policy Directive for Security Sector Assistance,[4] and congressional pressures make it likely that improvements will continue. But without OSD leadership, these efforts will remain ad hoc, and the results of improved AME will be almost impossible to regularize and aggregate in a manner useful for security cooperation planning and management at various levels or for coordination and collaboration with security sector assistance partners outside of DoD. Failure to create a DoD-wide AME system will result in security cooperation planning that lacks sufficient feedback mechanisms and

---

[4]   White House Office of the Press Secretary, *Fact Sheet: U.S. Security Sector Assistance Policy*, April 5, 2013.

rigorous, evidence-based analysis. Even well-designed plans may be undermined by poorly designed security cooperation activities, inconsistent application of best practices and continuous learning, poorly informed resourcing decisions, and failure to achieve strategic unity of effort. Incomplete or inconsistent AME will also impede the ability of senior officials to understand partner nation absorptive capacity, sustainability, and alignment of U.S. and partner interests.

The findings and recommendations in this report should help OSD provide the necessary leadership to accomplish the desired goals, primarily through more robust guidance, increased engagement inside and outside DoD, and a solid analytic framework.

Acknowledgments

We greatly appreciate the assistance provided by our sponsor, Deputy Assistant Secretary of Defense for Security Cooperation Tommy Ross, and his team, particularly Leslie Hunter, Ron Meyers, and Eileen Cronin. They and their OSD and Joint Staff colleagues provided important insights throughout our research.

We also recognize the invaluable contributions of those experts we interviewed at several DoD CCMDs, particularly PACOM and EUCOM. These include officials in PACOM's J45, J5, J8, and J9 and in EUCOM's J5/J8 and J7. We would like to thank the staff at the Department of State, USAID, and MCC who took the time to speak with us about their organizations' experiences with AME as well. In addition, we very much appreciate the feedback we received at our workshop on AME framework development from representatives of OSD, the Joint Staff, the DSCA, and the service headquarters and secretariats, among others.

We also thank our reviewers, Jennifer Moroney and Cynthia Clapp Wincek, whose feedback greatly improved this report.

Finally, we are grateful for the administrative support provided by Betsy Kammer and Theresa DiMaggio.

Abbreviations

AME   assessment, monitoring, and evaluation

CCMD   combatant command

CCP   Country Cooperation Plan or Country Campaign Plan

CDCS   Country Development Cooperation Strategy

CLO   country-level objective

CSCP   Country Security Cooperation Plan

DEEP   Defense Education Enhancement Program

DIB   defense institution-building

DIILS   Defense Institute of International Legal Studies

DIRI   Defense Institutional Reform Initiative

DoD   U.S. Department of Defense

DSCA   Defense Security Cooperation Agency

DTRA   Defense Threat Reduction Agency

ERR   economic rate of return

EUCOM   U.S. European Command

FMF   Foreign Military Financing

FY	fiscal year
GPOI	Global Peace Operations Initiative
GPOL	Global Partnering Opportunity List
GPRA	Government Performance and Results Act
G-TSCMIS	Global Theater Security Cooperation Management Information System
HQDA	Headquarters, Department of the Army
IEG	Independent Evaluation Group
IMET	International Military Education and Training
IMO	intermediate military objective
ISAF	International Security Assistance Force
ISSAF	Interagency Security Sector Assessment Framework
JCISFA	Joint Center for International Security Force Assistance
LOA	line of activity
LOE	line of effort
M&E	monitoring and evaluation
MACOM	major command
MCC	Millennium Challenge Corporation
MoDA	Ministry of Defense Advisors
MfR	Managing for Results
MOE	measure of effectiveness
MOP	measure of performance
NATO	North Atlantic Treaty Organization

NDRI	RAND National Defense Research Institute
OECD	Organisation for Economic Co-operation and Development
OPR	office of primary responsibility
OSD	Office of the Secretary of Defense
PACOM	U.S. Pacific Command
PCA	Partner Capability Assessment
PPD 23	Presidential Policy Directive for Security Sector Assistance
SAF/IA	Undersecretary of the Air Force for International Affairs
SAS	Strategy for Active Security
SCD	Systematic Country Diagnostic
SCO	security cooperation organization
SFA	security force assistance
SLOE	supporting line of effort
SMART	specific, measurable, achievable, relevant and results-oriented, and time-bound
SME	subject-matter expert
SSA	security sector assistance
TCP	theater campaign plan
USAID	U.S. Agency for International Development
WBG	World Bank Group
WIF	Wales Initiative Fund

CHAPTER ONE

Introduction

The U.S. Department of Defense (DoD) has spent billions of dollars annually on security cooperation, conducting three to four thousand events with over 130 countries each year executed by many different organizations, including combatant commands (CCMDs), services, and defense agencies, using military personnel, government civilians, and contractors. Security cooperation has several basic goals whose prominence varies, depending on current U.S. strategic and operational objectives and the partner nation that is being engaged. These goals include building the capacity of partner security forces to improve the security environment, strengthening relationships with foreign militaries and governments, securing access for U.S. military forces so they can more effectively operate abroad, and sharing information and intelligence with our allies and partners. Security cooperation activities range from the expensive and visible—training, equipping, and exercising together—to low-key but valuable bilateral talks, workshops, personnel exchanges, and professional military education.

At a time when the United States is increasingly relying on foreign partners for its security and attempting to build their military capacity, it is inappropriate to justify security cooperation activities and expenditures using only anecdotal evidence. In order to gauge security cooperation's "return on investment," senior leaders in the presidential administration and Congress are requesting a rigorous accounting of what is being done, spent, achieved, and not achieved in relation to specific planning objectives across the security cooperation enterprise.[1] Despite the keen interest of policymakers to understand the impact of DoD's security cooperation efforts, however, DoD has lacked effective guidance governing security cooperation assessment, monitoring, and evaluation (AME), as well as a common and tested AME framework.[2]

AME Purposes Include Accountability, Learning, and Determining Return on Investment

The purposes DoD identifies for AME within its security cooperation enterprise will frame how its policy and framework are ultimately shaped, balanced, and resourced and how the process and its results are expected to impact DoD. For example, organizations focused on achieving better results are likely to have a strong monitoring process closely linked to program implementation. Agencies focused on transparency and learning seek to conduct their planning, assistance, and AME with colleagues' and partners' participation. Those prioritizing accountability may have a strong financial bent to their AME.

Accountability (i.e., good stewardship of resources) is one of the most cited purposes for AME within the U.S. government and beyond.[3]

---

[1]   Jeremy Ravinsky, "The Pentagon's Security Assistance Wasteland," *thehill.com*, November 11, 2015.

[2]   *Assessment* is often used as a catchall term to describe some or all facets of AME. In this report, it refers primarily to the initial assessment of the security environment that provides the basis for subsequent measurements of security cooperation progress. *Monitoring* is a continuous process to gauge the extent of progress toward the achievement of security cooperation tasks and objectives that is often executed by those responsible for managing a program or activity, and *evaluation* is a formalized process generally conducted periodically or at the end of a program or activity, often by an outside agency, to ascertain the value of that program or activity in terms of its outcome, impact, or cost-effectiveness. A more extended definitional discussion can be found later in this chapter. We also attempt to parse components of AME more finely in the description of our proposed AME framework for security cooperation in Chapter Four.

[3]   For example, see United States Mission to the United Nations, "UN Transparency and Accountability Initiative," undated; and U.S. Government Accountability Office, *High-Risk Series: An Update*, Washington, D.C., GAO-15-290, February 2015.

While the Government Performance and Results Act (GPRA) and the GPRA Modernization Act reaffirmed a commitment to accountability, they also helped the federal government to shift the locus of its decisionmaking from activities to the results and implications of those activities.[4] This has enabled U.S. agencies to expand their orientation to include learning ways to improve project design and implementation (U.S. Agency for International Development [USAID])[5] and achieving more effective outcomes (Department of State and USAID).[6] International organizations applying best practices in AME also favor building more effective programs (the United Nations) and learning about what works in what context (the World Bank).[7]

AME focused on learning seeks to improve an organization's understanding of what works and why during implementation, as well as on deepening analysis at institutional (programmatic, strategic planning, and policy) levels over the longer term. Learning requires careful consideration of the processes, assumptions, and variables that should be monitored and evaluated in support of an organization's goals and objectives. Monitoring improves understanding and adaptability at the individual, operating unit, and policy levels. Independent, grounded evaluations that include a learning component provide an analytical perspective when determining what works in existing planning, design, and program implementation processes in terms of improving outputs and outcomes and what changes should be considered for subsequent programs, plans, policies, or business models.

---

[4] White House Office of Management and Budget, Government Performance Results Act of 1993; and GPRA Modernization Act of 2010.

[5] U.S. Agency for International Development, *Performance Management Plan (PMP) Toolkit, A Guide for Missions on Planning for, Developing, Updating, and Actively Using a PMP,* Washington, D.C., October 2013.

[6] U.S. Department of State and U.S. Agency for International Development, *FY 2015 Joint Summary of Performance and Financial Information,* 2015. USAID's Policy Bureau issues the Program Cycle Guidance (ADS200 series); although it is oriented toward improving project design and implementation, it is equally results-oriented.

[7] World Bank Independent Evaluation Group, *World Bank Group Impact Evaluations: Relevance and Effectiveness,* 2012.

AME focused on measuring and improving return on investment is a powerful tool for strategic decisionmaking, including resource allocation in support of current and future programs and activities. A standardized AME regimen applied across activities helps policymakers and implementers make more informed decisions that maximize immediate outcomes and help ensure programmatic sustainability and impact in the longer term.

Although the thrust of the AME effort is still being determined within the Office of the Secretary of Defense (OSD) and the Joint Staff, there are indications of the direction in which important elements of DoD would prefer to head. Interviews conducted by officials in OSD in 2015 with security cooperation stakeholders, decisionmakers, and practitioners throughout DoD and within relevant interagency circles[8] on their priorities for AME revealed an overwhelming concern with informing better outcomes now and improving future policy and programs, closely followed by improving utilization of security cooperation as a tool and informing resource allocation decisions.

DoD Needs a Common Definition for AME

Aside from choosing which AME purpose to emphasize, DoD must also ensure that security cooperation stakeholders are talking about the same thing when it comes to AME. In other words, it is not advisable for different DoD components to develop their own terminology, as this only generates confusion among stakeholders. At this point, several organizations within DoD have proposed measurement terms for use in the security cooperation realm. For example, in its Planning Guide, the Joint Center for International Security Force Assistance (JCISFA) states: "assessment is the continuous monitoring and evaluation of the current situation and progress of a joint operation

[8]   Interview counts were as follows: 17 from DoD, three from the Department of State/USAID, two at the senior policy decisionmaker level, four senior policy action officers from the Joint Staff, three policy action officers, four from program management, three program implementers, one defense attaché, three from budget, and two AME experts.

toward mission accomplishment."[9] The Joint Staff was also developing a definition of assessment as part of its deliberations on new guidance for security cooperation.[10]

In its discussions with stakeholders, OSD has sought to use terms that were in common use by other U.S. agencies. OSD officials describe "initial assessment" as the front-end analysis of the relevance, feasibility, and potential sustainability of a security cooperation plan, program, or activity conducted before implementation and of the conditions that may hinder its execution. Initial assessments focus on environment, capabilities, security cooperation tools, risks, and benefits. Baseline information resulting from these assessments shapes the initial monitoring and evaluation (M&E) questions and reference points that must be incorporated into security cooperation planning to ensure credible and feasible results. According to some officials, the initial assessment should be updated as warranted by the changing security and political context.[11]

From the perspective of some OSD officials, monitoring is an internal management responsibility conducted during implementation.[12] Substantively, it is an ongoing analysis of progress designed to provide regular feedback on achievement of planned activities and results, with the purpose of improving management decisionmaking and providing consistent reporting. Monitoring for security cooperation addresses the near-term implications of learning and accountability and focuses primarily on program performance, challenges for implementation, and financial accountability while tracking whether desired results are occurring. Monitoring focuses on performance, including outputs, milestones, unintended outcomes, obstacles, and costs.

In contrast, some OSD officials depict evaluation as a rigorous, independent analysis of the effectiveness, relevance, and sustainability of a security cooperation activity and its design, implementation,

---

[9]   JCISFA, *SFA Assessment Handbook*, Ft. Leavenworth, Kan., 2016.

[10]   RAND discussion with DoD officials, November 2015.

[11]   RAND discussion with senior OSD official, February 2016.

[12]   RAND discussion with senior OSD official, February 2016.

or results.[13] Evaluation may occur at a selected midpoint, at the end, and/or aftercompletion of a plan or program. Evaluations address the medium- to long-term implications of learning and return on investment and serve as a basis for informing decisionmaking on improving outcomes, process, and/or design, primarily for future iterations or efforts. Evaluation focuses on effectiveness including outcomes, cost-effectiveness, unintended outcomes, best practices, and lessons learned for the security cooperation enterprise.

There are multiple types of evaluation that can be conducted, depending on the nature of the project studied and the type of questions to be answered about the project. Impact evaluation may be thought of as the most scientific style of evaluation because it requires "a credible and rigorously defined counterfactual to control for factors other than the intervention that might account for the observed change."[14] This is appropriate for testing the underlying assumptions of a program: For example, to ascertain whether the education of girls contributes to poverty alleviation, researchers might study two very similar villages when only one implements an education program for girls. If the two villages have divergent poverty levels in the years after the education program is implemented, one may be able to assume that girls' education contributes to poverty alleviation in this case. This style of evaluation tends to be expensive, lengthy, and not well-suited to all types of foreign assistance programs.

Impact evaluations are not the only method for understanding the impact of a project. Performance evaluation is another way to understand the impact of assistance efforts, asking "what a particular project or program has achieved . . . how it is being implemented, how it is perceived and valued, whether expected results are occurring," and other outcome-related questions.[15] This evaluation style generally includes before-and-after comparisons and requires that decisions are made about how to measure success prior to implementation of the project. While not the scientific hypothesis-testing used in impact

---

[13] RAND discussion with senior OSD official, February 2016.

[14] USAID, "USAID Evaluation Policy," Washington, D.C., January 2011a, p. 2.

[15] USAID, 2011a.

evaluations, a well-defined performance evaluation provides rigorous study of project outputs and outcomes. Because they are more flexible, less expensive, and may be faster, performance evaluations are more common than impact evaluations.

In sum, monitoring focuses on whether desired results are occurring during implementation and confirms whether implementation is on track, whereas evaluation helps one to understand why a change occurred and whether there were unintended consequences, positive or negative.

DoD AME Must Conform to Higher-Level Guidance

Section 1202 of the 2016 National Defense Authorization Act required DoD to develop a strategic framework to guide prioritization of security cooperation resources and activities. A major component of this framework is "a methodology for assessing the effectiveness of Department of Defense security cooperation programs . . . including an identification of key benchmarks."[16] In addition to Congress's interest in using AME to improve its oversight, DoD security cooperation activities involve a plethora of stakeholders across the U.S. government. Signed in 2013, the Presidential Policy Directive for Security Sector Assistance (PPD 23)[17] mandates an inclusive and deliberate approach to how the U.S. government conducts business regarding security sector assistance (SSA), outlining roles, responsibilities, and requirements for federal departments and agencies. In particular, PPD 23 introduces requirements for AME for SSA stakeholders to promote unity of effort within and across agencies, focus resource alignment, improve strategy development, and inform future budget decisions. These requirements include the following:

---

[16]   National Defense Authorization Act for Fiscal Year 2016.

[17]   White House Office of the Press Secretary, *Fact Sheet: U.S. Security Sector Assistance Policy*, April 5, 2013.

- designing country- and regional-level plans with security sector components to facilitate M&E over the course of implementation
- establishing standards for uniform and integrated M&E of SSA, including guidance that objectives are outcome-based, achievable, measurable, and tied to stated assumptions
- appropriately funding M&E—to include the necessary assessment and planning activities required for quality M&E results.

To integrate consistent M&E principles and approaches, PPD 23 calls for SSA stakeholders (i.e., the Department of State and DoD) to develop (1) a framework that captures performance and results, featuring small baskets of indicators that, when combined, provide clarity on the outcomes of the U.S. government activities and policy;[18] (2) M&E for SSA that is consistent with established U.S. legislative requirements, standards and policies, and the incorporation of international best practices;[19] (3) a mechanism to feed analysis and learning back into the decisionmaking process; and (4) a midterm performance evaluation that allows for midcourse correction or adaptation.

DoD Faces Challenges to Developing a Comprehensive AME Structure

DoD has some of the building blocks in place to implement PPD 23 and maintain a leadership role in designing and achieving strategic security objectives. By early 2016, for example, OSD and the Joint Chiefs of Staff had established policy guidance to the geographic CCMDs requiring (1) initial assessments of security challenges and security sector conditions to serve as a baseline for designing security

---

[18] PPD 23 specifies two categories of indicators: (1) performance measures to measure progress toward security sector objectives and (2) a suite of contextual (strategic and capability) indicators that complement performance data by providing insight on relevant political, military, social, and economic factors related to SSA programming.

[19] Examples include the GPRA Modernization Act of 2010 and Organisation for Economic Co-operation and Development (OECD), *OECD DAC Handbook on Security Sector Reform: Supporting Security and Justice*, February 25, 2008.

cooperation activities and (2) evaluations of ongoing and completed security cooperation activities to determine the effectiveness of security cooperation programs. DoD already undertakes security cooperation AME, but it does so sporadically. Different program offices employ different AME approaches; they are frequently innovative, but their generalizability is uncertain.[20]

DoD faces an array of challenges in developing a comprehensive AME structure. One challenge will be creating a common methodological and terminological framework to guide AME across the entire security cooperation enterprise, consisting of 172 programs managed by multiple offices, agencies, and commands under the loose oversight of OSD, the Joint Staff, and the Department of State.[21] Another will be to develop initial assessments that identify the nature of the prob-

---

[20] RAND has published a number of studies in recent years on AME efforts being pursued by a variety of organizations within DoD engaged in security cooperation activities. For example, see Walter L. Perry, Stuart E. Johnson, Stephanie Pezard, Gillian S. Oak, David Stebbins, and Chaoling Feng, *Defense Institution Building: An Assessment*, Santa Monica, Calif.: RAND Corporation, RR-1176-OSD, 2016; Christopher Paul, Brian J. Gordon, Jennifer D. P. Moroney, Lisa Saum-Manning, Beth Grill, Colin P. Clarke, and Heather Peterson, *A Building Partner Capacity Assessment Framework: Tracking Inputs, Outputs, Outcomes, Disrupters, and Workarounds*, Santa Monica, Calif.: RAND Corporation, RR-935-OSD, 2015; Larry Hanauer, Stuart E. Johnson, Christopher Springer, Chaoling Feng, Michael J. McNerney, Stephanie Pezard, and Shira Efron, *Evaluating the Impact of the Department of Defense Regional Centers for Security Studies*, Santa Monica, Calif.: RAND Corporation, RR-388-OSD, 2014; Jennifer D. P. Moroney, David E. Thaler, and Joe Hogler, *Review of Security Cooperation Mechanisms Combatant Commands Utilize to Build Partner Capacity*, Santa Monica, Calif.: RAND Corporation, RR-413-OSD, 2013; Jennifer D. P. Moroney, Beth Grill, Joe Hogler, Lianne Kennedy-Boudali, and Christopher Paul, *How Successful Are U.S. Efforts to Build Capacity in Developing Countries? A Framework to Assess the Global Train and Equip "1206" Program*, Santa Monica, Calif.: RAND Corporation, TR-1121-OSD, 2011; Jennifer D. P. Moroney, Aidan Kirby Winn, Jeffrey Engstrom, Joe Hogler, Thomas-Durell Young, and Michelle Spencer, *Assessing the Effectiveness of the International Counterproliferation Program*, Santa Monica, Calif.: RAND Corporation, TR-981-DTRA, 2011; and Jennifer D. P. Moroney, Joe Hogler, Jefferson P. Marquis, Christopher Paul, John E. Peters, and Beth Grill, *Developing an Assessment Framework for U.S. Air Force Building Partnerships Programs*, Santa Monica, Calif.: RAND Corporation, MG-868-AF, 2010.

[21] These include programs found in Title 10 (Armed Forces), Title 22 (Foreign Relations and Intercourse), and Title 50 (War and National Defense) of the U.S. Code. For an analysis of DoD Title 10 security cooperation authorities and programs, see David E. Thaler, Michael J. McNerney, Beth Grill, Jefferson P. Marquis, and Amanda Kadlec, *From Patchwork to*

lem that needs to be addressed. It will also be challenging to determine whether security cooperation activities have contributed to U.S. objectives and, if so, by how much or in what ways. Because security cooperation activities are dispersed (mostly in complex environments) and often support long-term objectives, they are difficult to measure. Although those who plan and execute security cooperation may believe intuitively that the programs they manage have had the desired effect with respect to the partner nations they are engaging, they find it difficult to demonstrate this sense of progress empirically to higher-level decisionmakers. From a planning standpoint, the challenges will be to develop inclusive information on activities and resources that can be aggregated by country, program, and function;[22] standardized planning hierarchies; objectives that are specific, measurable, attainable, relevant and results-oriented, and time-bound (SMART); and country road maps that contain milestones and associated activities and performance measures.[23]

Framework: A Review of Title 10 Authorities for Security Cooperation, Santa Monica, Calif.: RAND Corporation, RR-1438-OSD, 2016.

[22] Although this is the impetus behind the Global Theater Security Cooperation Management Information System (G-TSCMIS), it has yet to be realized.

[23] See Michael J. McNerney, Jefferson P. Marquis, S. Rebecca Zimmerman, and Ariel Klein, *SMART Security Cooperation Objectives: Improving DoD Planning and Guidance*, Santa Monica, Calif.: RAND Corporation, RR-1430-OSD, 2016. Alternative definitions of SMART abound. They include the following (from D. T. Wade, "Goal Setting in Rehabilitation: An Overview of What, Why and How," *Clinical Rehabilitation*, Vol. 23, No. 4, April 1, 2009, p. 294):

- specific, significant, stretching, simple, stimulating, succinct, straightforward, self-owned, self-managed, self-controlled, strategic, sensible
- measurable, meaningful, motivational, manageable, magical, magnetic, maintainable, mapped to goals
- agreed upon, attainable, achievable, acceptable, action-oriented, attributable, actionable, appropriate, ambitious, aspirational, accepted/acceptable, aligned, accountable, agreed, adapted, as-if-now
- realistic, relevant, reasonable, rewarding, results-oriented, resources are adequate, resourced, recorded, reviewable, robust, relevant to a mission
- time-based, timely, tangible, trackable, tactical, traceable, toward what you want, and many other terms starting with "time-" (e.g. -limited, -constrained, etc.).

Based on RAND's prior research, we believe that SMART objectives are the foundation upon which an effective AME system is built and that any effort to improve AME would benefit from a simultaneous effort to improve how DoD planners develop security cooperation objectives. RAND's 2016 report on building SMART objectives (McNerney et al., 2016) analyzes these challenges and serves as a companion piece to this study.

DoD also faces the challenge of having to build a security cooperation workforce skilled in AME. This will require an initial infusion of expertise, as well as a path for building a sufficient knowledge base within the security cooperation workforce to manage and leverage these processes. To appropriately resource AME, DoD will also need to consider funding sources and stewardship and conduct budgetary analysis to determine the level of resources needed.[24]

Study Objective and Approach

This brings us to the role of this study in furthering the development of security cooperation AME. Charged with the responsibility for prioritizing, integrating, and evaluating security cooperation activities and aligning them with defense strategies and resources, OSD has sponsored a number of initiatives designed to improve department-wide planning and assessment of security cooperation efforts. In support of one of these initiatives, OSD asked the RAND National Defense Research Institute (NDRI) to recommend options for establishing an AME regime for DoD security cooperation.

The study team's approach to this request had two principal components: (1) an analysis of existing planning and AME processes and practices inside and outside DoD to understand what works and what does not in different contexts and (2) the construction of a conceptual framework that explains how AME methods might be applied, inte-

---

[24] Although the geographic CCMDs are a crucial nexus for AME, current budget cuts have reduced their capability. For example, the U.S. Southern Command previously had 25 people focused on AME; it now has four.

grated, and implemented by major security cooperation organizations so that they conform as closely as possible to analytic best practices and existing DoD policies, plans, and processes. Although our analysis focused on DoD-managed (Title 10) security cooperation programs, we envisioned a framework that would accommodate security assistance (Title 22) programs managed by the Department of State but implemented by DoD. To execute this approach, the team

- reviewed CCMD security cooperation planning and AME processes
- analyzed other relevant DoD and non-DoD AME practices
- developed and tested a DoD-wide AME framework for security cooperation
- identified key findings and recommendations for implementing the proposed framework.

These research tasks involved documentary analysis, interviews with subject-matter experts (SMEs) inside and outside DoD, and a workshop involving security cooperation officials in the capital region. RAND's interviews for this project were conducted with a human subjects protection protocol, and those individuals interviewed provided their personal views and did not speak for their respective agencies.

Reviewing CCMD Security Cooperation Planning and AME Processes
Our review of security cooperation planning and AME in the geographic CCMDs, which is the subject of Chapter Two, had two objectives: (1) to describe and compare security theater cooperation processes and (2) to determine the extent to which policy ends at the theater level are linked to country objectives and associated program activities and resources. This involved analyzing security cooperation planning documentation pertaining to the U.S. Africa Command, the U.S. Southern Command, the U.S. Central Command, the U.S. Pacific Command (PACOM), and the U.S. European Command (EUCOM). For EUCOM and PACOM, we conducted in-person and telephone interviews with security cooperation program officials in these commands and examined security cooperation program activities recorded

in DoD's Global Theater Security Cooperation Management Information System (G-TSCMIS) in several countries in each command that received significant security cooperation resources and had relatively clear security cooperation objectives. This review included DoD-managed programs and DoD-executed programs that are managed by the Department of State. EUCOM and PACOM were selected as the focus of our comparative CCMD analysis, in part, because of their diverse and numerous security cooperation activities and also because of their well-developed and significantly different planning and AME frameworks. Consequently, they offer robust and distinct alternatives to consider when building a DoD-wide system. Our review of other CCMD planning documents and their reporting in G-TSCMIS indicated that the extent of their objective-activity-resource linkages does not differ greatly from those reported by EUCOM or PACOM.

Analyzing Other Relevant DoD and Non-DoD AME Practices

As described in Chapter Three, the research team investigated AME practices being employed by DoD security cooperation organizations outside the geographic combatant commands, as well as by security and development assistance organizations outside of DoD. To do this, we developed a list of AME practitioners in consultation with the sponsor, selecting for analysis those that represented a range of large and diverse organizations in the foreign assistance realm with well-documented AME practices. Based on the availability of previous in-depth RAND research and the suggestions of our sponsor and DoD SMEs, we chose cases from the U.S. Army and Air Force, as well as from several major DoD security cooperation programs, including Section 1206/2282 train and equip and defense institution-building programs. In addition, following the advice of our sponsor and non-DoD experts on SSA M&E, we examined AME processes at the Department of State and USAID, as well as at the Millennium Challenge Corporation (MCC) and the World Bank. We analyzed and synthesized documents and studies related to these organizations' practices and conducted in-person and telephone interviews with AME practitioners to understand the characteristics of various AME processes, as well as their advantages and disadvantages. In our literature review and interviews, we covered topics related to the purpose and structure of AME systems, integration of AME into planning and program design, the feasibility of AME practices, and organizations' adherence to well-recognized evaluation principles.

Developing a DoD-Wide AME Framework for Security Cooperation

Chapter Four describes how we developed our proposed DoD-wide AME framework for security cooperation. This was accomplished by first considering the pros and cons of existing DoD and non-DoD AME processes based on data gathered from our case studies and from RAND and other assessment research. We then constructed a "straw man" AME framework that combined the strong points of current AME processes with best practices derived from the scientific literature. This framework consisted of two basic parts: (1) a general description of how AME should fit within DoD's existing security cooperation planning, resourcing, and implementation cycle and (2) a more detailed exposition of the major elements in an integrated AME system for security cooperation: focus areas, roles and responsibilities of major security cooperation stakeholders, key means of transmitting AME guidance and results, possible new AME organizations and processes, and costs incurred in fielding an integrated AME framework. The framework analysis also included an approach to prioritizing AME efforts to more effectively manage costs and workload.

In November 2015, OSD and RAND NDRI jointly hosted a workshop at RAND's Arlington, Virginia, office with security cooperation experts from the Washington, D.C., area—including officials from OSD, the Joint Staff, the four service headquarters, the Department of State, and nongovernmental organizations—to discuss the major elements of the proposed framework within the context of real-world security cooperation efforts. Subsequently, we also contacted security cooperation officials in EUCOM and PACOM via telephone and email to gather their views on the framework. We asked the D.C. workshop participants and CCMD officials to consider such questions as:

• Where should DoD focus its AME efforts?

- Who should be responsible for DoD AME guidance, management, data collection, and analysis?
- How and how often should AME results be transmitted?
- Is a centralized organization needed for AME? If so, where should it reside?
- What additional resources would be needed to execute an integrated AME framework?
- How should DoD prioritize its AME efforts?

The study team collected and compiled the responses to the above questions from workshop participants and CCMD officials. We then discussed proposed modifications to the straw man framework with our sponsor in OSD Security Cooperation and made adjustments when there was mutual agreement that those adjustments were desirable in order to incorporate AME into the existing security cooperation planning, resourcing, and implementation cycle; align security cooperation AME with best practices inside and outside of DoD; and/or achieve buy-in from important security cooperation stakeholders.

Finally, the team tested the revised AME framework by applying it to a notional case. In this exercise, we considered how the framework would be operationalized at various organizational levels and sought to identify assumptions, challenges, inconsistencies, and gaps in the framework. The example case focused on U.S. security cooperation efforts aimed at assisting the development of the maritime security capability of a fictitious country.

Identifying Key Findings and Recommendations for Implementing an AME Framework

Based on the research and analysis outlined above, Chapter Five identifies key findings and recommendations for the establishment of an effective, DoD-wide security cooperation AME framework and proposes improvements to OSD policy AME guidance that match the expectations of major security cooperation stakeholders within DoD.

CHAPTER TWO

Combatant Command Planning and AME

To a large extent, the geographic CCMDs serve as the linchpin for DoD's security cooperation efforts. Although they receive strategic guidance from OSD and the Joint Staff and resources and support from the services and the Defense agencies, the CCMDs are responsible for integrating the various components of security cooperation in order to help build relationships and capabilities of regional partners, improve interoperability, and secure operational access in close cooperation with U.S. embassy country teams. Consequently, we turn first to an examination of CCMD planning and AME before focusing on AME processes and practices at other DoD and relevant non-DoD organizations.

This chapter reviews the security cooperation planning guidance at CCMDs and analyzes the connections between objectives and programmed activities and resources. The goal of this analysis was to determine the extent to which policy ends at the theater level are linked to country objectives, as well as associated program activities and resources. To determine the robustness of the planning structure supporting theater campaign and country security cooperation AME, the research team took a two-pronged approach. First, the team mapped and qualitatively evaluated the linkages at the policy, CCMD, country, and event levels, as evidenced in OSD, EUCOM, and PACOM guidance. Then the study team quantitatively analyzed the linkages using G-TSCMIS data from fiscal year (FY) 2014.

Planning and Evaluation of Security Cooperation by EUCOM and PACOM

Each CCMD follows its own internal process in planning and evaluating security cooperation. This section describes the planning and AME processes used by EUCOM and PACOM for their theater campaign plans (TCPs) and country plans and the nexus between them based on interviews with responsible officials on the CCMD headquarters staffs in 2015 and on observations made in our review of each CCMD's planning documents. EUCOM and PACOM represent only two of DoD's six geographic CCMDs, but both have mature and significantly different planning and AME frameworks. Our review of other CCMD planning documents and their reporting in G-TSCMIS indicated that their security cooperation activities and the objective-activity-resource linkages in their planning do not differ greatly from those reported by EUCOM or PACOM.

At the time of our research (spring 2015 to spring 2016), each CCMD was in the process of updating its TCP, based on the latest OSD planning guidance. In the discussion that follows, we note any intended changes to the processes, as revealed during interviews conducted with CCMD staff later in 2015.

U.S. European Command

Every two years, EUCOM produces an updated theater strategy that serves as the command's road map for engagement activities in the coming years.[1] This document identifies the EUCOM commander's priorities, which are in accordance with but derived separately from OSD planning guidance. These priorities are expressed as lines of effort (LOEs).

The EUCOM TCP unifies OSD planning guidance and the EUCOM commander's strategy and identifies intermediate military objectives (IMOs) for each OSD planning guidance end state.

---

[1]   U.S. European Command, "J5/8—Policy, Strategy, Partnering and Capabilities," undated; the EUCOM theater strategy was previously called "Strategy for Active Security (SAS)," but in October 2015 it was renamed "theater strategy."

The TCP also generates supporting lines of effort (SLOEs) from the intersection of the commander's objectives, priorities, and LOEs. The EUCOM TCP also includes two regional campaign plans.

EUCOM Country Cooperation Plans Focus on Lines of Activity

It is through the country plan that the varying levels and types of guidance are harmonized. EUCOM's country plans, known as Country Cooperation Plans (CCPs), look out between two and five years and operationalize the commander's LOEs, each of which contains one or more lines of activity (LOAs) and typically references IMOs and OSD planning guidance end states. While the backbone for an LOA is the commander's guidance, national and other guidance also drive LOA development.

The LOA level may be considered the core of EUCOM's security cooperation work. EUCOM maintains a portfolio of 45 LOAs that possess standard verbiage and are included in the CCPs as needed.[2] While an LOE represents a broad goal, an LOA encapsulates a collection of country-specific outcomes, tasks, and activities within its respective topical domain. Each LOA is owned by a designated office of primary responsibility (OPR) that is the functional expert for security cooperation activities in that sphere. For instance, U.S. Naval Forces Europe is responsible for the maritime-related LOAs, and the EUCOM J6 oversees the Command, Control, Communications, and Computers and Cyber LOAs. The OPR is responsible for mapping the requisite outcomes, tasks, resources, activities, and events to support progress along the LOA.

EUCOM country cooperation plans take three forms. The country desk officers in the J5 directorate draft the CCP base plans, which identify country end states, LOEs, and LOAs. CCP roadmaps are unclassified versions of CCP base plans that are releasable to partner nation governments. Lastly, EUCOM maintains a version of the CCPs within its SAS plan, a database interface developed by EUCOM to

---

2   Interview with EUCOM headquarters officials, in-person interview with author, May 12, 2015.

manage security cooperation planning and activities.[3] The SAS plan depicts the nesting of outcomes, tasks, resources, activities, and events under the LOAs and SLOEs. The database serves as a live repository for security cooperation that is more detailed than what appears in either the CCP base plan or the CCP roadmap documents. It maintains a record of each country plan as it changes over time. The SAS plan system has some functional overlap with G-TSCMIS, but it appears to have greater utility as a planning tool that shows the nesting of activities and events under objectives.

Linkages Among EUCOM's Security Cooperation Policy Objectives and Program Activities and Resources Are Not Fully Apparent

Figure 2.1 maps the linkages from OSD planning guidance end states through programed activities and events, based on our independent review of EUCOM's planning documents. The gray arrows indicate how elements of higher planning strata drive lower elements. The green arrows indicate references that lower strata make to higher strata. Lastly, the black arrows indicate how activities and events are tied to the specific objectives, according to our review of G-TSCMIS entries.

Three Findings from Mapping EUCOM Linkages

The mapping exercise yielded three potential disconnects in the EUCOM security cooperation planning process, as highlighted by the blue circles. These include the following:

1. Inconsistency among the three versions of the EUCOM CCPs (base plan, roadmap, and SAS database) in terms of which higher-element LOAs are linked. In the 2014 base plans and roadmaps we reviewed, LOAs fall under specific LOEs. In this case, LOAs, activities, and events do not link directly to OSD planning guidance end states. From briefs and interviews with EUCOM planners, LOAs fall under specific SLOEs in the SAS database. In this case, activities and events do link to OSD planning guidance end states.

---

[3]   SAS plan stood for "Strategy for Active Security Plan," but that term is no longer in use.

Figure 2.1
Linkages Among EUCOM's Objectives and Program Activities

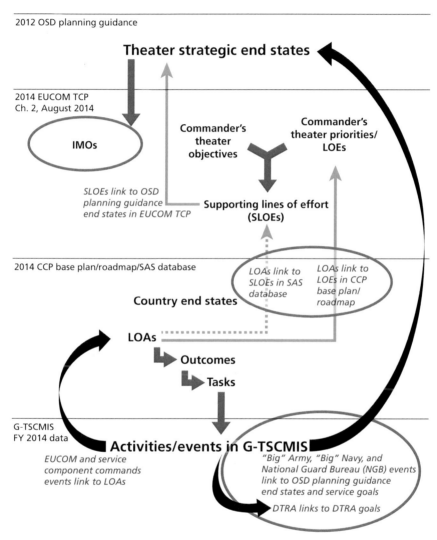

2. In G-TSCMIS, event owners cite their activities and events as
    supporting different objectives. EUCOM and service CCMDs
    tie events to EUCOM LOAs. "Big" Army (e.g., Headquar-
    ters, Department of the Army [HQDA], U.S. Army Training
    and Doctrine Command), "Big" Navy (e.g., Naval Education
    and Training Command), and the National Guard Bureau tie
    their events directly to OSD planning guidance end states. The
    Defense Threat Reduction Agency (DTRA) ties its events to
    DTRA-specific objectives.[4]
3. Lastly, while LOAs may make reference to EUCOM's OSD
    planning guidance end state supporting IMOs, there is no
    direct linkage from activities and events to IMOs.

Evaluation of Security Cooperation Objectives at EUCOM Is Largely Subjective

Evaluation of security cooperation objectives at EUCOM is centered
on an annual LOA progress report and maintained in the SAS plan.
The LOA progress report is a largely subjective look at progress toward
the LOA. It contains a narrative and color-coded assessments, with
green meaning on track, yellow meaning off track but results still
achievable, and red meaning off track.[5] The narrative portion of the
progress report includes sections for current status, results, hindrances
to accomplishment, and strategy and plan considerations.[6] While the
progress report is written by the OPR, it is reviewed by the embassy-
based senior defense official/security cooperation officer and approved
by the EUCOM country desk officer.[7]

The EUCOM J7 Assessments division integrates these LOA progress reports with political and military analysis to generate country and
thematic assessments. In addition to this level of assessment, the J7

---

[4] It was observed that, beginning in FY 2015, DTRA tied events to EUCOM LOAs.

[5] Interview with EUCOM headquarters officials, in-person interview with author, May 13, 2015.

[6] Perry et al., 2016, p. 133.

[7] Interview with EUCOM headquarters officials, in-person interview with author, May 13, 2015.

also prepares the comprehensive joint assessment for EUCOM, part of a common process across the CCMDs to assess progress toward OSD planning guidance objectives and IMOs.[8]

U.S. Pacific Command

PACOM officials develop and prioritize the command's LOEs and IMOs based on the end states provided by OSD planning guidance. Besides the OSD planning guidance, PACOM planners also utilize other functional and regional strategy documents to refine their IMOs and develop specific effects and tasks.[9]

The 2014 version of the PACOM TCP contains 170 IMOs and looks out over a five-year period.[10] Most PACOM IMOs are not country-specific, but there are exceptions. The IMOs are bundled into 11 LOEs. Two of the LOEs (allies and partners and all hazards) contain most of PACOM's security cooperation–related IMOs and effects. Every component of the TCP is prioritized, from LOEs to IMOs to effects to strategic tasks.[11]

PACOM J5 country managers develop partner end states and country objectives based on the LOE/IMO/effects roadmap, which are incorporated into country pages within the TCP.[12] Country pages are intended to address a range of issues of interest to PACOM, including security cooperation.[13]

---

[8] Interview with EUCOM headquarters officials, in-person interview with author, May 13, 2015.

[9] Interview with PACOM headquarters official, phone interview with authors, February 20, 2015.

[10] During the period of our study (spring 2015 to spring 2016), J5 planners were working on the FY 2016–2020 version of the document. They also indicated that the command had taken an "appetite suppressant" while developing the current TCP and reduced the number of IMOs from 170 to 38 in the draft version.

[11] Interview with PACOM headquarters official, phone interview with authors, February 10, 2015.

[12] Interview with PACOM headquarters official, phone interview with authors, February 20, 2015.

[13] Interview with PACOM headquarters official, phone interview with authors, February 20, 2015.

PACOM Country Security Cooperation Plans Are Derived from the Top Down and the Bottom Up

PACOM's Country Security Cooperation Plans (CSCPs) are intended to synchronize security cooperation ways and means employed by security cooperation providers with the country objectives contained in the TCP, the partner nation's priority list, and the U.S. embassies' integrated country strategies. Although the PACOM J45 manages the CSCP generation process in coordination with the J5, it is the embassy-based security cooperation organizations (SCOs) that are responsible for writing these slide-based documents.[14] According to our interviews, SCOs are the primary vehicles for validating the plans against the partner nation's priorities and ensuring that capabilities are adequately resourced over a period of five years.[15] As a result, the partner capabilities described in the CSCPs are not always driven by an IMO in the TCP; sometimes an idea "bubbles up from the bottom" and a related IMO is subsequently developed.[16]

The PACOM CSCPs reviewed for this study were composed of country objectives taken from the TCP; a list of prioritized country capabilities and partner nation priorities; and a plan of events, activities, and investments over the next five years.[17]

Disconnects Among PACOM's Security Cooperation Policy Objectives and Program Activities and Resources

Figure 2.2 maps the linkages from OSD planning guidance end states through programmed activities and events, based on our independent review of PACOM's planning documents. The gray arrows indi-

---

[14] Interview with PACOM headquarters official, phone interview with authors, February 19, 2015.

[15] Interview with PACOM headquarters official, phone interview with authors, February 10, 2015.

[16] Interview with PACOM headquarters official, in-person interview with authors, April 8, 2015.

[17] The CSCPs presented at the May 2015 Theater Security Cooperation Working Group conference included five major elements: (1) country end states taken from the TCP, (2) priority LOEs, (3) prioritized capabilities and capacities, (4) an analysis of partner capability gaps, and (5) an "enduring employable capability roadmap."

Figure 2.2
Linkages Among PACOM's Objectives and Program Activities

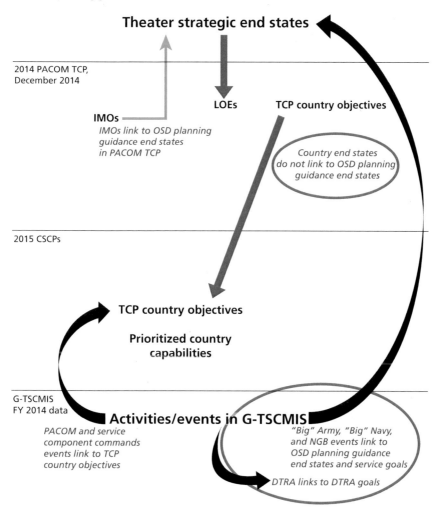

2012 OSD planning guidance

Theater strategic end states

2014 PACOM TCP,
December 2014

LOEs   **TCP country objectives**

IMOs

*IMOs link to OSD planning
guidance end states
in PACOM TCP*

*Country end states
do not link to OSD planning
guidance end states*

2015 CSCPs

TCP country objectives

**Prioritized country
capabilities**

G-TSCMIS
FY 2014 data   **Activities/events in G-TSCMIS**

*PACOM and service
component commands
events link to TCP
country objectives*

*"Big" Army, "Big" Navy,
and NGB events link to
OSD planning guidance
end states and service goals*

DTRA links to DTRA goals

cate how elements of higher planning strata drive lower elements. The green arrows indicate references that lower strata make to higher strata. Lastly, the black arrows indicate how activities and events are tied to the specific objectives, according to our review of G-TSCMIS entries.

Findings from Mapping PACOM Linkages

The mapping exercise yielded two potential disconnects in the PACOM security cooperation planning process, as highlighted by the blue circles. These include the following:

1. The country objectives identified in the PACOM TCP are not directly linked to TCP LOE, IMOs, or OSD planning guidance end states.

2. Similar to EUCOM, event owners cite different objectives for their activities and events in G-TSCMIS. PACOM and service CCMDs tie events to PACOM TCP country objectives. "Big" Army (i.e., Army organizations at the institutional level), "Big" Navy, and the National Guard Bureau tie events directly to OSD planning guidance end states. DTRA ties events to DTRA-specific objectives.[18]

The Process for Evaluating Security Cooperation Objectives at PACOM Is Under Development

PACOM's main AME focus is on evaluating the progress that the command is making with respect to the LOEs spelled out in its TCP. As Figure 2.3 illustrates, this LOE-based evaluation process is systematic and complex. IMOs are subdivided into a number of more specific effects, which represent environmental conditions resulting from an action or actions that contribute to IMO achievement. Effects are evaluated by measures of effects, generally qualitative criteria, and associated quantitative metrics called measures of effects indicators. Effects are further broken down into mission-essential tasks, which constitute the basic steps required to achieve effects. These strategic tasks are evaluated by measures of performance, resources required for mission accomplishment, and capability enablers known as measures of perfor-

---

[18]   It was observed that in FY 2015, DTRA tied events to PACOM TCP country objectives.

Figure 2.3
PACOM's LOE Evaluation Framework

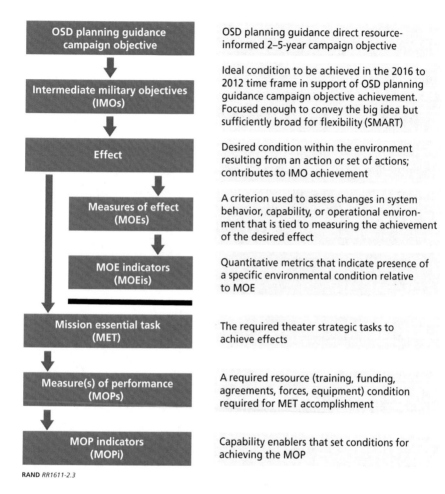

RAND RR1611-2.3

mance indicators. Interviewees indicated that this evaluation process had not yet been fully exercised. At the time of this study (spring 2015 to spring 2016), the process stopped at the effects level and did not include measuring effects and tasks via measures of effects and measures of performance, which were still under development.[19]

---

[19] Interview with PACOM headquarters officials, in-person interview with authors, April 7, 2015.

At present, TCP tasks are largely self-evaluated by those responsible for executing them. TCP planners generally rely on proxy qualitative measures rather than direct quantitative measures when doing evaluations of IMOs, particularly those that are "too large to measure quantitatively."[20] PACOM's approach includes red, yellow, and green "stoplight" objective assessment charts and SMEs' comments that the J83 synthesizes into a narrative.

While relying on G-TSCMIS to provide a common operating picture of security cooperation activities, PACOM has developed a separate web-based monitoring mechanism, the Strategic Management System, to keep track of LOE objectives, effects, tasks, and measures.[21]

The AME process associated with the CSCP is less structured and mature than the theater campaign process. SCOs are largely responsible for assessing partner country needs and evaluating progress in filling capability gaps.[22]

Conclusion

As illustrated by experiences of EUCOM and PACOM, the CCMDs have taken important steps toward improving security cooperation planning and AME, but there are still gaps and areas for improvement. EUCOM has developed customized tools for prioritizing the many objectives in this complex area of operations, as well as a customized system for tracking progress toward objectives. However, the connections between country and theater planning elements are inconsistent, and there is no direct path from security cooperation activities and events to IMOs. In the area of AME, processes are nearly all based on self-assessment or the counting of very basic event-level data. While

---

[20] Interview with PACOM headquarters officials, in person interview with authors, April 7, 2015.

[21] Interview with PACOM headquarters officials, in-person interview with authors, April 7, 2015.

[22] Interview with PACOM headquarters official, phone interview with authors, February 20, 2015.

rigorous in its design, the system lacks a way to consistently test security cooperation hypotheses or analyze outcomes.

PACOM has recently made significant improvements in the way it conducts security cooperation planning and AME. In particular, by reducing the number of IMOs, the command has made the 2015 version of its TCP easier to understand and utilize for AME than the previous plan. In addition, PACOM has a well-developed framework for evaluating IMOs associated with its major LOEs. In spite of these improvements, the connections among theater campaign planning, security cooperation country planning, and AME are not as tight as they could be. Another shortcoming is PACOM's AME process for security cooperation. Despite the effort to simplify its TCP, the way it conducts AME is complex and does not extend to the country level.

As Chapter Three shows, the AME processes and practices at other DoD and relevant non-DoD organizations are, in some ways, more advanced than those found in the CCMDs. However, they also have their weaknesses, and their usefulness for the development of an integrated security cooperation framework must be carefully evaluated.

Analysis of Relevant AME Frameworks

The challenge of assessing, monitoring, and evaluating international engagements and assistance is not unique to DoD's security cooperation efforts. Under various names, the notion of understanding program efficacy is central to how organizations learn and grow. In developing guidelines for good practice in security cooperation AME, it is helpful to review case studies representing several other AME systems that may be relevant. For the purposes of this research, we have selected cases from the U.S. Army and Air Force and select DoD security cooperation programs that highlight a diverse range of positive AME practices. In addition, USAID and the Department of State form key U.S. government cases outside DoD that have strong applicability to security sector assistance. Finally, MCC and World Bank represent cases of bilateral and multilateral foreign assistance programs with detailed AME systems. We chose these cases based on the availability of previous in-depth RAND research and the suggestions of our sponsor and DoD SMEs. Our cases allowed us to analyze a diverse set of good AME practices for a wide range of missions. Because they face similar AME challenges—e.g., working with foreign partners, complex security environments, information aggregation—their lessons were relevant for security cooperation. Within DoD, we analyzed practices from both military service and DoD-wide program perspectives. Beyond DoD, we analyzed two agencies often directly involved in security cooperation work and two other organizations with mature yet still innovative AME approaches.

While not an AME system in itself, OECD does have a set of principles that codify best practices for evaluation—using a broad definition of the term—and to which a number of international organizations work to comply. It also has a widely used security sector reform handbook that highlights evaluation and other best practices. Experts in the United States and internationally use OECD's handbook and leverage OECD as a forum for discussing how to implement its evaluation principles and refine their approaches.

In general terms, the purpose of evaluation in OECD's guidelines is to improve future policy and programming and to provide accountability. The general principles by which good evaluation works to do this are

- impartiality and independence: separation of evaluation from line management
- credibility: expertise and transparency
- usefulness: answer the right questions at the right time
- evaluation programming: must be planned, resourced, and staffed, not ad hoc; leaders set priorities and guidelines
- design and implementation: each evaluation has a statement of work with purpose, methods, standards, budget, and dissemination plan
- reporting, dissemination, and feedback: broadly accessible, improve future plans
- participation: donors and recipients are consulted and informed
- donor cooperation: donors collaborate to facilitate learning.[1]

In general, this exploration of case studies finds that AME systems do not tend to treat each aspect of AME equally. Leaving aside definitional ambiguity, most systems tend to focus on either assessment or evaluation. Monitoring is usually treated as an ongoing and sometimes automatic process, which perhaps accounts for the failure to describe it in detail. Within the military, evaluation most often con-

---

[1]   Development Assistance Committee, "Principles for Evaluation of Development Assistance," Paris: Organisation for Economic Co-operation and Development, 1991.

sists of self-evaluation and is fairly limited in terms of measuring outcomes. With respect to assessment, regional and country assessments are typically part of the military operations planning process. The civilian world, however, places a heavy emphasis on evaluation. While the military is apt to call the whole of AME "assessment," nonmilitary institutions often use "evaluation" as a catchall term. This means that assessment is often treated as a programming step, and M&E specialists are not involved. In contrast, the civilian institutions profiled here all have evaluation policies, many of which are quite detailed.

The following sections outline selected cases and discuss their possible relevance to DoD security cooperation AME.

Selected DoD AME Frameworks Separate Assessment from Monitoring and Evaluation

Army and Air Force Country Assessments Show Diverse Processes[2]
Introduction and AME Systemic Considerations

The military services tend to define assessment broadly. The Army, for example, sees assessment as an aspect of each phase of the operations process: i.e., planning, preparation, and execution.[3] In this respect, security cooperation differs very little from wartime or other contingency operations: In the mission assessment phase, planners consider various factors in the security cooperation environment when developing objectives; in the concept assessment phase, programmers ensure that processes, programs, and activities are aligned with security cooperation objectives; and in the execution assessment phase, those responsible for implementing security cooperation programs and activities monitor and evaluate their results in terms of relevant objectives.

Although service personnel are involved in each of the three assessment phases, the Army and Air Force have focused their institu-

---

[2]   The information for this case was collected through discussions with current and former DoD officials and DoD contractors supporting security cooperation assessments in 2010–2011 (Army) and 2015–2016 (Air Force).

[3]   Department of the Army, FM 5-0, *The Operations Process*, March 2010.

tional efforts on the initial phase. Specifically, HQDA and the Undersecretary of the Air Force for International Affairs (SAF/IA) have in recent years each designed and, to a certain extent, implemented processes for assessing the level of capability exhibited by a wide range of U.S. partner nations in the land and air/space domains—as well as other country characteristics, such as interoperability with the United States and the quality of relationships with the United States—in order to provide a service perspective on future security cooperation needs and priorities.

Army's Continuum Assessment

By the mid-2000s, building the capacity of partner country security forces had become a major goal of the U.S. Army. To facilitate this goal, the international affairs division within the operations and planning staff (G-3/5/7) of HQDA proposed a process for assessing the connection between a partner's military capability/capacity and interoperability with the United States, existing building partner capacity (BPC) programs, and U.S. objectives with respect to BPC in target countries. To implement this, the Army developed the Army Security Cooperation Continuum assessment framework. As envisioned in 2006–2007, the purpose of the continuum was to provide U.S. Army security cooperation planners with a rough assessment of the ground force capacity and interoperability of every significant country in the world. It is important to note that the decision to measure interoperability was a subjective Army choice, and there are many factors upon which to assess and evaluate partnership capacity. Relying on in-person facilitated discussions with groups of SMEs from the Army Staff and the major commands (MACOMs), G-3/5/7 plotted countries in a linear fashion along a vertical interoperability axis and a horizontal capability axis.

The G-3 chose to construct the interoperability axis of the continuum framework first. Drawing on the existing body of standards developed by the North Atlantic Treaty Organization (NATO) and American British Canadian Australian allies, G-3 developed a detailed scorecard to enable SMEs to assess the interoperability of a country's ground forces with the U.S. Army. This scorecard was based on six major components of interoperability: command, inform, deploy, operate, protect, and sustain. In practice, command and operate were used to establish distinctions at lower levels of the interoperability scale while inform, deploy, protect, and sustain were more relevant for distinguishing among countries at the higher end of the scale. For example, a country's army was defined as Level 0 if the U.S. Army had not engaged with it in more than two years and the two armies' command and control could only interact at the national level. In the case of a Level 3 country, networks enabled shared situational awareness and functional integration at the brigade level and below with respect to all six interoperability components.

In 2007, HQDA G-3 also developed a concept for the capability/ capacity axis of the continuum framework that was never converted into a detailed worksheet or tested with SMEs or partner countries. At the left end of this notional axis were security importers that required outside assistance to maintain their territorial integrity and/or internal stability. Further to the right were security exporters that possessed more ground force capacity than necessary to protect against internal or external threats and, therefore, could potentially contribute forces to out-of-area military missions. The extent of a security exporter's capability was based on the size and range of its potential contributions to international operations. Specifically, SMEs were asked to push each country's army through a three-stage analytical filter consisting of the following questions:

1. Can a foreign army contribute to international operations?
2. Can a foreign army contribute multiple combat battalions and/ or substantial combat support/combat service support to international operations?
3. Can a foreign army contribute a brigade or more, self-deploy, and make forced entry on demand?

According to G-3's concept, answering these three questions would provide sufficient information to assign every country to one of four levels of capability.

Air Force's Partner Capability Assessment

Although the Army's continuum assessment process stalled for reasons that are discussed in the following subsection, SAF/IA has more recently developed and begun to implement a more detailed process for assessing the air, space, and cyber capabilities and relationships of a range of U.S. partners (currently, 91). The Partner Capability Assessment (PCA), a survey-based tool administered by SAF/IA's strategy division, has been executed twice in somewhat different forms in 2013 and 2015. The PCA is derived from data primarily provided by Air Force country desk officers at SAF/IA and the air component commands within the geographic CCMDs and secondarily from SMEs in the Air Force's major commands. Its results are used as inputs to the Air Force's Global Partnering Opportunity List (GPOL), which serves as a guide to capability maximization and risk mitigation for the Air Force. The target audiences for the GPOL include U.S. embassy country teams and CCMDs responsible for establishing partner country security cooperation objectives, as well as Air Force regional components and Air Force headquarters strategy and operations staffs that determine ways to achieve security cooperation objectives.

A partner country's overall relative PCA standing is based on a combination of its capability and relationship scores, which are in turn derived from an aggregation of capability and relationship subcategory scores. (As a result, partners are characterized as being high capability/low relationship, high capability/high relationship, low capability/low relationship, or low capability/high relationship.) Partner capabilities assessed in 2015 include air superiority; strike; mobility; intelligence, surveillance, and reconnaissance; command and control; and agile combat support. Each capability is associated with a unique set of subcategories. To determine a subcategory score, SAF/IA averages the responses from a varying number or Air Force organizations to a series of binary and rubric questions and combines the results based on complex weighting scheme. Rubric questions—for example, those dealing with subcategories of air superiority—require respondents to determine a partner's standing based on a combination of number of assets, level of proficiency, and extent of interoperability with the USAF.

Relevance for DoD Security Cooperation AME from Army and USAF Frameworks

If fully implemented, service partner country capability/interoperability assessments have the potential to directly provide useful information to security cooperation planners and programmers who lack domain expertise or service perspectives on what is needed from partner militaries. Receptive audiences would seem to include country desk officers in CCMDs and component commands and security cooperation officers in U.S. embassies responsible for security cooperation planning and activity development. To this point, however, neither HQDA nor SAF/IA has established a systematic process for injecting service partner country assessments into joint and interagency planning and programming. This is one reason why the Army's continuum assessments have never had much practical impact and why the Air Force's PCAs will likely face the same fate—unless they can break out of their intraservice "bubble."

The structure of the continuum's capability/capacity axis also limited its utility. A multidimensional attribute, ground force capacity includes both hardware components, such as equipment and units, and software components, such as doctrine and training. HQDA G-3's original concept focused mostly on the size of partner contributions to coalition operations (the hardware aspect of capacity). Although G-3's concept did not completely neglect the software aspect, it conflated force size, deployability, and sustainability, making it impossible to independently measure these different components of capacity. In addition, a rigorous comparison of foreign armies requires specifying the context in which their ground forces are being employed. In other words, "capacity for what" is a critical issue for assessment. G-3's concept gave short shrift to a country's capacity to counter domestic security threats, concentrating instead on its ability to contribute to international operations. Such a focus inhibited the Army's understanding of potential partner requirements for defeating or deterring domestic insurgents, terrorist networks, or hostile neighbors.

In contrast, SAF/IA's survey-based assessment has the potential to provide a much more detailed picture of partner capabilities within the air, space, and cyber domain. However, the PCA also has structural and procedural limitations. Although it simplifies assessment administration and facilitates comparative analysis, a standardized survey instrument, mostly organized in accordance with USAF functions and doctrine, may not be the best way to assess capabilities and relationships that pertain to very different types of partners that are of varying interest to the United States. Also, the PCA survey's heavy reliance on complex, rubric-based questions not only makes it impossible to independently assess certain partner attributes, such as interoperability, but it also may be responsible for the high variability of responses in important capability categories of the 2013 assessment. Finally, as was the case with the continuum assessment, the current PCA is almost entirely dependent on qualitative data collected from a limited number of SMEs. It is doubtful whether this is the best method for gathering factual capability or relationship information, such as the number of partner assets or the existence of a cooperative agreement. Furthermore, SAF/IA and component desk officers, who currently furnish most of the PCA's data, may not always be the best source of information on specific aspects of partner air force proficiency, and simply averaging their responses, without providing an adjudication or quality control mechanism, leaves one less than confident in the assessment's accuracy.

DoD's Section 1206/2282 Train and Equip Program Shows Some Rigor[4]
Introduction and AME Systemic Considerations
Within DoD, the Assistant Secretary of Defense for Special Operations and Low Intensity Conflict oversees a promising evaluation process for its Section 2282 (formerly Section 1206) Train and Equip program.

In 2004, the Secretary of Defense directed his staff to pursue additional authorities from Congress to help foreign militaries quickly respond to emerging security threats. After intense negotiations within the executive branch and extensive discussions with Congress, the FY 2006 National Defense Authorization Act provided the authority for

---

4   The information for this case was collected in January and March 2016 through discussions with current and former DoD officials and DoD contractors supporting the program.

the Section 1206 Train and Equip program, which was repealed and replaced by Section 2282 in December 2014.

Designed to build the capacity of foreign militaries to conduct counterterrorism and stability operations, it was the first global train and equip authority for DoD since the Foreign Assistance Act of 1961 gave authority over security assistance to the Department of State. The Section 1206 program had similarities with the Department of State's Foreign Military Finance program and thus created significant concerns among some stakeholders in the Department of State, National Security Council Staff, and Congress. The Secretary of Defense took a personal stake in the success of the program, however, believing that this new authority would help DoD be more agile, particularly with its counterterrorism efforts. Ultimately, the program successfully took root, and it now provides up to $350 million in assistance per year to numerous countries.

Since the original FY 2006 act, with some updates in subsequent years, Congress has required a robust AME structure. As shown in Table 3.1, the law mentions assessments in five places.

With the advent of an annual congressional reporting requirement in FY 2012, OSD set up a more rigorous AME system. From 2012 to early 2016, DoD conducted AME events in over 20 countries. In addition to meeting a congressional reporting requirement, the Section 2282 AME system provided an opportunity for DoD's own leadership to get better visibility into this large and high-visibility program.

The overall AME process is founded on a theory of change, as shown in Figure 3.1, expressed as a logic model—a concept also used by USAID. USAID applies logic models to all sectors of assistance, such as health and education. While the logic model shown could be applied to most train and equip activities, DoD could also develop standard logic models based on other common capability development areas, such as military-to-military contacts and engagements, exercises, professional military education, and institution-building.

DoD has documented its Section 1206/2282 AME approach in a handbook to ensure consistency of application. Because they occur at different points of the year, results of AME trips informally feed into programming cycles. While there is still room for improvement, AME

Table 3.1
Section 1206/2282 AME Requirements

Requirement	Description
Congressional notification requirements	A description of the program objectives and assessment framework to be used to develop capability and performance metrics associated with operational outcomes for the recipient unit
	An assessment of the capacity of the recipient country to absorb assistance under the program
	An assessment of the manner in which the program fits into the theater security cooperation strategy of the applicable geographic CCMD
Assessment funding	Amounts available to conduct or support programs under subsection (a) shall be available to the Secretary of Defense to conduct assessments and determine the effectiveness of such programs in building the operational capacity and performance of the recipient units concerned.
Reporting requirement added as of FY 2012	An assessment of the effectiveness of the program in building the capacity of the foreign country to conduct counterterrorism operations during the fiscal year covered by such report, and a description of the metrics used to evaluate the effectiveness of the program
	A description of the procedures and guidance for monitoring and evaluating the results of programs under this section

SOURCE: DefenseAssistance.org, "Underlying Law for Defense Budget Aid Program: Authority to Build the Capacity of Foreign Security Forces," undated.

is becoming increasingly relevant as the system becomes more transparent to stakeholders. The details of the AME reports are not shared with the partner nation, to protect confidentiality of interviewees. In one case, however, a report was mistakenly provided, which led to positive results. Interviewees in a partner nation refused to provide information, so the team recommended no further assistance. Some time later, the partner nation saw the report, apologized, and became much more forthcoming with information.

Assessment

As with many AME efforts, the Section 1206/2282 AME system was incorporated into a program that was already well under way, so the system was not designed with separate AME components. Many visits, therefore, include M&E of past efforts, combined with assessments for potential future investments. That said the Section 1206/2282 system (which is generally referred to as an "assessment process") does break down its work into baseline assessments, monitoring of outputs, and evaluations of outcomes.

DoD focuses on the partner nations and units—where the inputs in the logic model shown in Figure 3.1 are going—when defining assessments. As shown in Figure 3.2, they conduct their assessments of the partner country by looking at relevant capabilities ("what can they do?") and at performance missions the partner conducts ("what do they do?"). When assessing capabilities and performance, they look at whole systems, not just those components relevant to what DoD has provided or might provide.

To conduct its assessments, DoD uses a contract with a small team of independent outside evaluators working with DoD and embassy officials. The team will generally spend about a week meeting with partner

Figure 3.1
Logic Model Adapted for Section 1206/2282 Programs

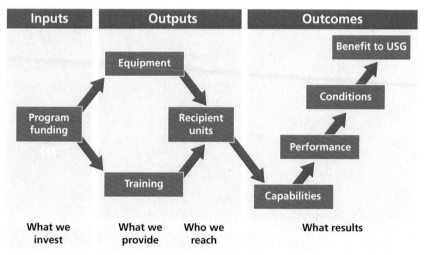

SOURCE: Science Applications International Corporation, *The Assessment Process for Section 1206 Global Train and Equip Programs*, briefing, October 2013.
NOTE: USG = U.S. government.
RAND *RR1611-3.1*

Figure 3.2
Section 1206/2282 Assessment Concept

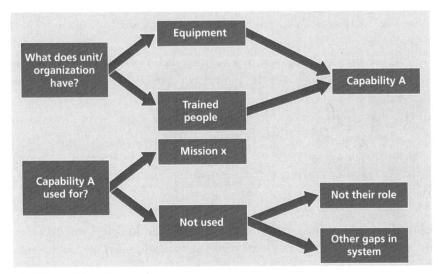

SOURCE: RAND analysis.
RAND RR1611-3.2

nation officials and recipient unit personnel. The baseline assessments address recipient unit capability and performance prior to receipt of 1206/2282 program equipment and training. The team uses five levels of capability and performance. They assess partner nation units according to reasonable standards for recipient nations, not by U.S. standards. These standards are applicable to all partner nations that receive assistance. They focus their assessments at the program level but sometimes comment more broadly on such items as the security environment and partner nation relations.

The outside evaluators, not DoD, are responsible for the assessment report. The relevant CCMD will provide the baseline assessment for any program proposal using forms provided by the outside evaluators, but for the data to be reliable, it is important that CCMD or embassy experts visit the partner nation unit. An OSD-led contracted evaluation team will conduct a trip one to three years after receipt of training and equipment. Assessments will focus on the unit to receive the equipment or training but will also look at other capabilities the partner nation has, including capabilities provided by others. The five levels of capability and performance mentioned above are described in Unit Type Assessment Frameworks developed by SMEs for each of the following capability categories and selected others:

- land
- border security
- land special operations
- counterinsurgency
- maritime
- naval special warfare
- maritime patrolling
- maritime surveillance
- air
- strike
- airlift
- air surveillance and reconnaissance.

Given limited program resources, OSD would like to focus the external team on M&E, leaving assessments to CCMDs and embassies.

Monitoring

Using the logic model above, the 1206/2282 team focuses on the "outputs" when defining monitoring.[5] Was the equipment delivered to the recipient unit? Was the training completed? Is there evidence that the equipment or training is being put to good use? When the process was first initiated, OSD provided guidance that the CCMD would complete a program delivery report to confirm equipment arrival or training completion. Six months after the delivery report, the CCMD was expected to visit the unit to obtain evidence that the equipment or training was being used—for example, by observing the partner unit effectively exercising with the equipment on its own.

These reports were never completed as required. Thus, the independent evaluation team will often visit recipient partner organizations

---

[5]   Chapter One of this report discusses various definitions of monitoring.

about one year after training or equipment is provided to both monitor use of the assistance and evaluate the effects of that assistance. Although DoD has been somewhat satisfied with this approach, limited funds mean that if embassies and CCMDs could more reliably conduct the necessary assessments and monitoring, the independent evaluation team could focus more on evaluating outcomes, which is the ultimate goal of the AME system, as designed by 1206/2282 program monitors.

Evaluation

Using the logic model above, the 1206/2282 team focuses on the "outcomes" when defining evaluation. Evaluations can measure the outcomes of a program both to facilitate completion and to understand its overall impact once complete. Multi-year programs can use anecdotes to highlight areas of progress without ever understanding whether they achieved the desired effect at an acceptable cost.

For the evaluation process, the independent evaluation team travels to the partner unit one to three years after provision of equipment or training. Using the Unit Type Assessment Frameworks applied in the assessment phase, the team evaluates the progress of the unit within the framework's five levels of capability and performance. The independent team is responsible for the evaluation, collecting whatever data they can on the impact of the assistance: In what ways is the unit more capable? What improvements is the unit showing in its performance thanks to this assistance?

To help answer these questions, the evaluations are framed against one of 14 particular missions. The assistance should be improving capabilities that then result in improved tactical performance in particular missions that help to advance its security interests—and U.S. security interests—overseas. Thus, the outcomes should be able to show a clear link between improved partner capabilities and benefits to the United States. Evaluations are not yet consistently discussed at the start of DoD planning for future assistance, but the intent is to create stronger feedback loops to connect evaluations with future planning.

The results of evaluations are consolidated into an annual report that highlights key points for the Secretary of Defense to transmit to

Congress. In addition to using the reports to inform Congress, DoD also uses them to facilitate discussions across CCMDs and military services and with stakeholders outside DoD, particularly the Department of State.

One area that seems to work well is that the system is designed to be rigorous without being completely quantitative. The evaluation team conducts informal interviews with partners to elicit both strengths and weaknesses, while also looking for concrete evidence to validate interview data. Connecting these evaluations more formally to decisions about future investments is still a work in progress, however, as is the ability to understand how much of a partner unit's improvement is directly due to 1206/2282 assistance.

Relevance for DoD Security Cooperation AME

The 1206/2282 team judges its AME system—and the likely utility of other AME systems—in several ways. Is it focusing on priority countries? Is it focusing on priority goals? Is it focusing on areas most relevant to those goals? Is there an effective feedback loop? Can one make a causal link between the programs inputs and desired outcomes—i.e., are the programs actions supporting their theory of change? Another, perhaps underappreciated, way to judge an AME system is what the 1206/2282 team refers to as the "Hawthorne effect." Does the AME system motivate individuals to improve their performance in response to their awareness of being observed?[6]

Of interest to DoD security cooperation AME is the procedural clarity of the AME process, particularly the handbook that describes the system in detail. In addition, the logic model and the framing of evaluations determine progress toward one of a set of predetermined missions. These two aspects of 1206/2282 AME may help architects

---

[6]   Research on lighting and work structure changes at the Hawthorne Works, a factory in Illinois, was originally interpreted to mean that paying attention to overall worker needs would improve productivity. Later interpretations suggested that the novelty of being research subjects and the increased attention from such could lead to temporary increases in workers' productivity. This interpretation was dubbed the "Hawthorne effect" (R. McCarney, J. Warner, S. Iliffe, R. van Haselen, M. Griffin, and P. Fisher, "The Hawthorne Effect: A Randomised, Controlled Trial," *BMC Medical Research Methodology*, Vol. 7, No. 30, 2007).

of a DoD-wide system to provide conceptual clarity and a degree of systematization, while preserving enough flexibility to serve the varied range of security cooperation goals to be found DoD-wide. Another interesting aspect of this AME system was the funding of the effort through a portion of its annual congressional funding appropriation. One potential concern we identified was that evaluators might ask questions typical of an impact evaluation, in terms of identifying causal links between improved performance of units and improved conditions for the partner nation, but without the level of data rigor and counterfactual evidence that would typically be required in a methodology for impact evaluation. This creates the potential for "false positives," in which attribution of change in a country may be given to a program simply because evaluators are looking for evidence of a link. The evaluation team, however, mitigates this risk by deliberately avoiding trying to establish exclusive causality between the outcome of a given 1206/2282 program and changed conditions in the partner nation and by trying to identify other factors that may influence outcomes.

Defense Institution-Building AME Is Different for Different Programs

Introduction and AME Systemic Considerations

One major obstacle in assessing, monitoring, and evaluating DIB programs is that DIB activities can be sporadic, making long-term measurement and the understanding of impact a difficult task.[7] Additionally, AME functions may be carried out at three different levels, each with their own tracking mechanisms (the DIB planner level, the CCMD level, and the Regional Center level). Historically, DIB has been implemented through five separate programs: the Wales Initiative Fund (WIF), the Defense Institutional Reform Initiative (DIRI), the Defense Institute of International Legal Studies (DIILS), the Ministry of Defense Advisors (MoDA) program, and the Defense Education Enhancement Program (DEEP).[8] The DIB AME process, though con-

---

[7]   See Perry et al., 2016, p. 91

[8]   The Wales Initiative Fund was formerly known as Warsaw Initiative Funds. See DSCA, "Warsaw Initiative Funds (WIF)," undated(b).

ducted differently between programs and among CCMDs, ultimately plays a role in understanding whether intended DIB activities are providing the desired outcome in the partner nation.[9] The purpose of this section is to understand AME practices within each DIB program.[10]

Generally, each DIB program manager monitors activity progress either through OSD liaison officers posted within CCMDs or through interim partner nation visits.[11] DIB activities, along with other security cooperation programs' activities, are tracked through G-TSCMIS and the Concept and Funding Request databases.[12] Both databases provide a qualitative metric that is used in determining future program funding and course corrections as needed.[13] Both DIB program planners and CCMD staff evaluate DIB activities based on partner nation end states stipulated in CCMD TCP objectives.[14] Table 3.2 outlines where DIB functions occur within each CCMD.

The next sections outline the current AME processes for each of the DIB programs.

Wales Initiative Fund—Defense Institution-Building (WIF-DIB)

The WIF's goal is to support NATO's Partnership for Peace, Mediterranean Dialogue, and the Istanbul Cooperation's Initiative to "develop more professional and transparent defense establishments" within selected partner nations.[15] Some objectives of the program include supporting the development of effective ministries of defense and

---

[9] For more robust security sector reform assessment definitions, see N. Popovic, *Security Sector Reform Assessment, Monitoring & Evaluation and Gender (Tool 11)*, Geneva Centre for the Democratic Control of Armed Forces (DCAF), 2008.

[10] See Perry et al., 2016, for a thorough explanation of assessment at the CCMD level.

[11] RAND CCMD interviews conducted during FY 2014–FY 2015.

[12] Defense Security Cooperation Agency, *Operation and Maintenance, Defense-Wide Fiscal Year (FY) 2016 Budget Estimates*, February 2015.

[13] For a more detailed description of the event databases, see Perry et al., 2016, pp. 130–135.

[14] As stated in CCMDs TCPs.

[15] U.S. Government Accountability Office, *NATO Partnership: DoD Needs to Assess U.S. Assistance in Response to Changes in the Partnership for Peace Program*, Washington, D.C., GAO-10-1015, September 2010, p. 10.

Table 3.2
DIB Functions by CCMD

CCMD	Planning	Implementation	Assessment
U.S. Central Command	J5	J5	J5
U.S. Special Operations Command	J55	J55	J8
U.S. Southern Command	J9	J9	J73
PACOM	J45	J45	J45
U.S. Africa Command	J5	J5	J1/8
EUCOM	J5	J5	J7

SOURCE: Perry et al., 2016.

increasing transparency and accountability in personnel and resourcing systems.[16] As such, AME functions here will eventually serve to understand whether such objectives are being met at the partner nation level. However, WIF-DIB program planners have yet to define assessment. Rather, AME occurs as part of a "deliberative" planning process that attempts to align WIF-DIB outcomes with the selected country LOAs.[17] Efforts to fully implement AME functions and tasks are ongoing.[18]

Defense Institute Reform Initiative (DIRI)

DIRI, implemented in FY 2010, provides "direct support for partner nation efforts to develop accountable, professional, and transparent defense establishments that can manage, sustain, and employ their forces and the capabilities developed through U.S. security cooperation programs."[19] Although DIRI now has a clearly defined mission set and goals, program and activity performance measurement still

---

[16]   For a more thorough review of WIF-DIB objectives, see Perry et al., 2016, p. 136.

[17]   Perry et al., 2016, pp. 137–138.

[18]   RAND interviews at CCMDs, FY 2015.

[19]   Defense Security Cooperation Agency, *Fiscal Year 2013 Budget Estimates*, February 2012a, p. DSCA-435.

vary, according to the CCMDs.[20] In previous RAND research on DIB programs, researchers found that evaluation of DIRI programs was included as part of the yearly overall CCMD AME process.[21] A consistent AME process has yet to be implemented across CCMDs for measuring DIRI progress. The DIRI program created "institutional capability categories," breaking each capability area into component parts—for example, human resource management included recruiting, accession, assignment, and retention. These parts were then broken down further, such that illustrative measures of effectiveness could be designed for each. Rather than trying to develop standardized indicators, the DIRI program focused on understanding the desired impact, identifying the theory of change to achieve that impact, and collecting information to validate the theory or make adjustments.

Defense Institute of International Legal Studies (DIILS)

DIILS leads DoD security cooperation efforts for "global legal engagement and capacity building with international defense sector officials through resident courses and mobile programs."[22] DIILS accomplishes this through resident program courses and mobile engagement teams. AME functions under DIILS are mostly qualitative; while DIILS publishes an annual report listing accomplishments for country engagement (such as participants served, curriculum developed, and legal frameworks adopted), the program has not yet focused on long-term outcomes that can be effectively assessed.[23]

Ministry of Defense Advisors (MoDA)

MoDA teams function under two headings: MoDA Afghanistan and Global MoDA. MoDA's mission for both is to partner "DOD civilian experts with foreign counterparts to build ministerial core compe-

---

[20] In FY 2012, the inspector general faulted DIRI for not having clearly defined sets of objectives or performance measures (Inspector General Report, "Defense Institution Reform Initiative Program Elements Need to Be Defined," 2012).

[21] Perry et al., 2016, p. 150.

[22] DIILS, *FY15 Annual Report*, 2016b, p. 4.

[23] See DIILS FY 2014 and FY 2015 annual reports (DIILS, 2016a and 2016b) for a full listing of country engagements.

tencies such as personnel and readiness, logistics, strategy and policy, and financial management."[24] As with DIRI, MoDA was faulted in FY 2012 with not providing adequate performance measures within the implementation of its programs in Iraq and Afghanistan.[25] Since then, OSD has been working to implement a performance framework that covers "program office responsibilities, including advisor recruiting, training, and deployment performance indicators."[26]

In Afghanistan, MoDA's assessment process has been stunted by existing International Security Assistance Force (ISAF) security force assistance (SFA) AME processes. The ISAF has adopted an SFA-based system in Afghanistan to "manage the transition from unit-based SFA to its new functionally based SFA role," establishing an SFA assessment process to support its functions.[27] ISAF's current assessment process has incorporated the creation of an SFA center to coordinate and synchronize the essential functions, daily and weekly reporting on progress, staff-assisted visits aimed at getting feedback directly from the Afghan Corps, monthly essential function reports, development of a problem-solving mechanism using problem sheets and a tracking matrix, and a program of activities and milestones designed to achieve ISAF essential functions' end states.[28] ISAF has precluded MoDA from developing its own assessment process. As such, MoDA has relied on the ISAF-instituted SFA process.

Outside of Afghanistan, Global MoDA mission planners control the assessment process, though defining DIB in small countries and finding qualified trainers to implement MoDA activities still prove dif-

---

[24] Defense Security Cooperation Agency, "Ministry of Defense Advisors Program," undated(a).

[25] Inspector General Report, "Performance Framework and Better Management of Resources Needed for the Ministry of Defense Advisors Program," DODIG-2013-005, October 23, 2012.

[26] Deputy Assistant Secretary of Defense for Partnership Strategy and Stability Operations, "Performance Framework and Better Management of Resources Needed for the Ministry of Defense Advisors Program," Memorandum for the Director, Joint and Southwest Asia Operations, Office of the DODIG, August 31, 2012 (as cited in Perry et al., 2016, p. 144).

[27] Perry et al., 2016, pp. 145–146.

[28] Perry et al., 2016, pp. 146–147.

ficult.[29] Despite these obstacles, Global MoDA AME frameworks have been implemented in several countries.[30] They involve (1) a country-needs assessment, (2) an execution plan, and (3) an evaluation plan.[31] Table 3.3 describes the AME process under each step.

Defense Education Enhancement Program (DEEP)

Although DEEP is a subprogram of WIF-DIB, its program managers use a separate set of AME processes to evaluate program effectiveness. This is because AME processes are fairly decentralized, and program managers have an understandable desire to tailor these processes for their own needs. Although there is value to tailoring AME processes, creating greater consistency might allow for more holistic evaluations of DIB by senior officials. DEEP's goal is to contribute to "international security through professionalization of the officer corps, NCO [noncommissioned officer] corps and civilian defense officials of partner countries, making their defense education institutions compatible with Western defense education standards and values."[32] DEEP's 13 partner

Table 3.3
MoDA AME Process

Country-Needs Assessment	Execution Plan	Evaluation Plan
• Advisors required to observe for the first 60 days of deployment • Idea is to identify areas needing reform • Areas are discussed with their host nation counterparts to secure agreement	• Action plan designed to implement the reforms • Must include milestones and host nation agreement	• Monthly reports evaluate progress toward reaching defined milestones

SOURCE: Perry et al., 2016, pp. 147–149.

---

[29] Perry et al., 2016, pp. 146–149.

[30] Perry et al., 2016, pp. 146–149.

[31] Global MoDA's evaluation plans are essentially self-reports on progress; they contain no contributions from agencies or independent observers (Perry et al., 2016, p. 149).

[32] Partnership for Peace Consortium, "Defense Education Enhancement Program," undated.

nation activities are evaluated based on eight measures of effectiveness (MOEs). To understand whether an activity has achieved one of the eight measures, DEEP program managers perform self-assessments based on observable qualitative metrics—such as whether, for example, new defense program curriculums have been implemented by the partner nation or whether Partnership for Peace countries have adopted a more Western-style defense organization.

Relevance for DoD Security Cooperation AME

The challenge of AME for DIB programs highlights the challenges that will be faced by rolling out a single AME framework for all security cooperation activities. The nature of DIB programs as sporadic, long term, and implemented by U.S.-based, rather than theater-based, personnel makes AME standardization and data collection difficult. However, within DIB programming, AME can most likely be further standardized—if not through common collection processes, then perhaps through a common logic model and mission set, as with Section 1206/2282 programs.

Nonmilitary AME Frameworks Provide Interesting Insights

This research utilizes case studies from several nonmilitary AME systems. First, we review U.S. Department of State AME, which includes, but is not limited to, security assistance M&E. Next we examine the USAID AME process. The remainder of the chapter discusses MCC and World Bank Group (WBG) AME.

Department of State AME Addresses a Diverse Range of Foreign Assistance Goals

Introduction and AME System

The Department of State framework for understanding program effectiveness is known as Managing for Results (MfR). The process appears to have grown out of a drive in the late 1990s to implement a strategic planning and performance management government-wide, which resulted in the Government Performance and Results Act.[33] In this sense, MfR is more than an AME tool; it is a comprehensive framework, to include budgeting and long-term planning, meant to guide the agency toward its strategic goals. In 2010, the Quadrennial Diplomacy and Development Review directed the Department of State to implement a streamlined strategic planning framework, as well as more robust M&E, under the banner of MfR.[34] This new framework (see Figure 3.3) is managed by the Office of U.S. Foreign Assistance Resources and the Bureau of Budget and Planning, using inputs from the operating units.

The MfR framework does not preclude more customized AME processes. In the area of security assistance, PPD 23 specifies additional AME measures.[35] In addition, previously existing Department of State security cooperation programs, such as the Global Peace Operations Initiative (GPOI), have varying degrees of robustness in AME functions.

Assessment

In the MfR framework, assessment falls under program planning. This mirrors the dichotomy between assessment and M&E seen in many other systems, including those in DoD. Assessment appears to exist on multiple levels within the Department of State, from the strategic level to the country level. Whereas the strategic-level planning leads to higher-level guidance, lower-level assessment is more apt to feed into program design, which could theoretically be linked explicitly to M&E formulation. Absent clear guidance for assessment and its integration into the AME process, many bureaus have developed templates for front-end assessments because they support getting baseline infor-

---

[33] U.S. General Accounting Office, *Managing for Results: Agencies' Annual Performance Plans Can Help Address Strategic Planning Challenges*, Washington, D.C., January 1998.

[34] U.S. Department of State, *Leading Through Civilian Power: The First Quadrennial Diplomacy and Development Review*, Washington, D.C., 2010, pp. 188–204.

[35] White House Office of the Press Secretary, *Fact Sheet: U.S. Security Sector Assistance Policy*, April 5, 2013.

Figure 3.3
Managing for Results Framework

RAND RR1611-3.3

SOURCE: Adapted from U.S. Department of State and U.S. Agency for International Development, *FY 2014 Annual Performance Report, FY 2016 Annual Performance Plan*, undated, p. 5.

mation.[36] The most frequently used types of assessments are technical in nature, aimed at providing definition and baselines to individual projects or programs. However, a recent evaluation of MfR implementation found that strong program design was lacking at the Department of State, indicating that assessment could be approached more rigorously.[37]

In contrast with larger Department of State policies, assessment is a required part of PPD 23 implementation. While those types of assessments vary, one helpful guide for an interagency security sector assessment in the public domain is USAID's Interagency Security Sector Assessment Framework (ISSAF), which has been utilized by Department of State–led security sector assistance programs, such as the Security Governance Initiative.[38] The ISSAF provides a multi-step process to identify capability and capacity shortfalls, barriers to change, and political will and to prioritize responses to these challenges.

Monitoring and Evaluation

As with other AME frameworks described in this study, the Department of State tends to combine monitoring and evaluation functions. As part of the MfR framework, the Performance Plan and Report process is intended to unify the M&E process by providing a standard table of indicators that may be reported on by operating units department-wide in a standardized reporting template. This is managed at the departmental level by the Department of State's Office of U.S. Foreign Assistance Resources and tied in most cases to functional bureau strategies and performance indicators. The performance indicators are attached to individual bureau objectives and bureau plans. However, the way this system is structured impedes the disaggregation of M&E-related

---

[36] Author interviews with Department of State and USAID M&E officials, March 17, 2016. One example is the Security Governance Initiative's "SGI Analysis Framework, Methodology, and Standard Operating Procedures."

[37] U.S. Department of State, "Evaluation of the Office of U.S. Foreign Assistance Resources' Implementation of the Managing for Results Framework," Washington, D.C., December 30, 2015b, pp. 6, 10.

[38] Chemonics International, "Interagency Security Sector Assessment Framework," Washington, D.C.: United States Agency for International Development, October 1, 2010.

data. This makes it difficult to budget for gathering evaluation data as opposed to monitoring data and has resulted in instances of spending on evaluations that do not correspond to their assigned budget because M&E efforts are not kept distinct.[39] The Department of State is working actively to improve this system, including by updating the Foreign Affairs Manual to encourage planning for monitoring before funds are spent on programs.[40] With respect to the implementation of PPD 23, monitoring is a specified activity.

In general, policies on evaluation tend to lead other aspects of AME. The Department of State has an evaluation policy and companion evaluation guidance which specify that:

> At a minimum, all bureaus and independent offices should undertake at least one evaluation per fiscal year. However, those who receive and directly manage program funds must conduct evaluations of their large programs once in their lifetime. Additionally, pilot programs should be evaluated before replicating.[41]

Per Department of State policy, evaluations may be conducted internally, externally, or collaboratively, so long as the evaluators are considered both qualified and impartial. Bureaus also maintain evaluation coordinators to facilitate the work of evaluation inside the Department of State. However, the recent evaluation of the implementation of MfR found that "several Bureau leaders reported not knowing off-hand the outcome of evaluations or whether recommendations were implemented."[42] The report suggested that updating evaluation guidance to strengthen feedback mechanisms would result in better, more relevant evaluations.

In the area of security assistance programming, M&E varies greatly by program and does not appear to be coordinated between

---

[39] Author interviews with Department of State and USAID M&E officials, March 17, 2016.

[40] Author interviews with Department of State and USAID M&E officials, March 17, 2016.

[41] U.S. Department of State, "Department of State Evaluation Policy," January 29, 2015a.

[42] U.S. Department of State, 2015b, p. 9.

programs, even if this would create efficiencies.[43] Programs in Foreign Military Financing (FMF) and International Military Education and Training (IMET) date back 40 years and have extended across 127 countries. However, because these undertakings have not generally been thought of as "projects," but rather as ongoing efforts, M&E have not generally been applied to FMF and IMET.[44] Program staff in 2016 were trying to reverse engineer evaluation processes by making explicit the logical framework underlying the programming.

The Global Peace Operations Initiative (GPOI) was the first of the Department of State's security assistance programs to develop M&E, and because of this, it has a robust system dating back to 2006. Monitoring and evaluation at GPOI focuses on answering five questions:

- Did the unit/individual deploy, sometime later, to a peace support operation?
- If they did deploy, were they effective?
- If the unit/individual did not deploy, were they employed in some activity/position which contributed to peace operations capabilities in their country?
- Can the unit, in a sustained manner, effectively train themselves?[45]

Within the program, there exists an M&E cell tasked with collecting data, conducting assessments, and identifying lessons learned.[46] Initially, M&E at GPOI was focused on collecting monitoring data and conducting five-year reviews of strategic plans, without rigorous documentation of outcomes, which are now becoming the focus.[47] The program is also working to answer questions of attribution, or the

---

[43] Author interview with Department of State officials, August 14, 2015.

[44] Author interview with Department of State officials, August 14, 2015.

[45] U.S. Department of State, "Global Peace Operations Initiative (GPOI): Program Monitoring and Evaluation," August 29, 2011.

[46] U.S. Department of State, 2011.

[47] Author interview with Department of State officials, August 14, 2015.

degree to which change in the country context can be credited to the programmatic intervention.

The Global Security Contingency Fund (GSCF) is a pilot program begun in 2012 to pool funding and integrate effort between Department of State and DoD staff. Within GSCF, M&E are intended to be "baked in from the beginning" and part of the programming over the life of any implementation.[48] A results framework (a document linking intermediate and final objectives to program goals) for the program was developed during its first year of existence, and this is applied to country programs through end-of-year evaluations, with the rest of M&E consisting of ongoing monitoring efforts.[49]

In the area of counterterrorism security assistance, the Department of State manages two programs, the Trans-Sahara Counterterrorism Partnership (TSCTP) and the Partnership for Regional East Africa Counterterrorism (PREACT). A series of 2014 U.S. Government Accountability Office (GAO) reports on the Department of State's counterterrorism programs found generally that TSCTP fulfilled the guidelines set out by PPD 23, but GAO found issues with monitoring of financial data, saying, "TSCTP's program managers may lack the day-to-day access to financial information that federal standards for internal control state is required to make operating decisions, monitor performance, and allocate resources."[50] With respect to PREACT, however, GAO found serious challenges to M&E, specifically:

> Presidential Policy Directive 23 highlights key factors—partner country needs, absorptive capacity, sustainment capacity, U.S. efforts, and other donor efforts—as critical to building partner capacity and focusing limited resources. [The Department of] State reported considering these key factors when selecting

---

[48] Author interview with Department of State officials, August 14, 2015.

[49] Author interview with Department of State officials, August 14, 2015.

[50] U.S. Government Accountability Office, *Combating Terrorism: U.S. Efforts in Northwest Africa Would Be Strengthened by Enhanced Program Management*, Washington, D.C., June 2014b, p. 1.

PREACT activities. However, State did not consistently document its consideration of the five factors.[51]

Further, the report found that the Department of State "does not have a comprehensive list of specific [PREACT] activities and has presented some information inaccurately in the bureau's Performance Plans and Reports."[52] Today, these programs have established M&E frameworks and baselines for data, but they acknowledge that acquiring data across the agencies with which the program works remains challenging.[53]

Relevance for DoD Security Cooperation AME

The Department of State and DoD share the need to manage a vast array of programming, along with a requirement to change not only guidance but also operational culture in order to do so. One of the Department of State's solutions to this problem has been to streamline reporting to a series of standard indicators and a common reporting portal that is in the process of being brought online. This experience offers both helpful guidance and cautions for DoD. The development of standard indicator tables provides a level of quasi-automation in the process that may make it vastly easier to collect relevant data from all operating units. However, devolving indicator reporting to that level likely requires some level of training and incentivization in order to provide quality inputs. This was identified in the MfR implementation evaluation document as a gap for the Department of State as well: "Missions and Bureaus have been implementing MfR processes and products, but without sufficient capacity, training, or a reward structure, implementation remains inconsistent."[54] In the case of the Department of State, the MfR report recommends that training be implemented at the Foreign Service Institute. However, without an analogous single

---

[51] U.S. Government Accountability Office, *Combating Terrorism: State Department Can Improve Management of East Africa Program*, Washington, D.C., June 2014a, p. 1.

[52] U.S. Government Accountability Office, 2014a, pp. 28–29.

[53] Author interview with Department of State officials, August 14, 2015.

[54] U.S. Department of State, 2015b, p 11.

training institution, this may be more difficult to roll out for DoD. The difficulty of gaining user acceptance for G-TSCMIS shows how challenging this could be in the case of DoD and how the utility of the overall effort will suffer if data entry is incomplete or inaccurate.

Next, the utilization of standard indicators can result in a diminished understanding of country context and country-specific program effectiveness. This is because the relative importance of specific indicators tends to vary across countries. For example, the creation of a doctrine for peacekeeping operations might be a particularly challenging target to reach in Country A, but an easy goal in Country B, dependent on the country's relative institutionalization of security governance. Equating the two would provide a certain ability to monitor program activities globally but would not substitute for a more tailored country- or project-specific evaluation. Thus, for DoD, the utility of such an approach becomes a question of costs versus benefits, since some form of tailored evaluation—likely narrative and qualitative—would still be required to identify lessons learned. This is the approach that Department of State security sector assistance programs are now taking, as a result of requirements outlined in PPD 23.

The United States Agency for International Development Has a Detailed AME Policy

In 2011, then-administrator of USAID Rajiv Shah announced a new evaluation policy intended to restore the agency's reputation as an evidence-based aid provider, saying:

> In 1994, USAID conducted nearly 500 independent evaluations. By the time I arrived, only 170 evaluations were submitted to Washington, despite a threefold increase in programs managed. In many instances, our project evaluations have been commissioned by the same implementing organizations that run the programs. Often, what passes for evaluation follows a two-two-two model. Two contractors spending two weeks abroad conducting two dozen interviews. For about $30,000, they produce a report

that no one needs and no one reads. And the results they claim often have little grounding in fact.[55]

To correct this, USAID's evaluation policy places a high degree of emphasis on planning for evaluations and integrating them into the program cycle for USAID projects, described in Figure 3.4.

One of the distinguishing features of the AME system is the high degree of specificity in roles and responsibilities for evaluation staff. The policy itself is a 20-page document that provides a single set of agreed-upon definitions for AME terms and makes explicit the roles and responsibilities of each sub-agency unit in the organization for AME.[56] While these roles and responsibilities are also included in the agency's formal policy and guidance documentation, having them in a single, easily accessible document increases their utility. USAID evaluation standards are intended to guide evaluation implementation (shown in Table 3.4).

A second distinguishing factor of the AME system as a whole is the commitment to training all USAID staff in AME: New staff are provided in-person training as part of the onboarding process, including such topics as stating a development hypothesis and developing indicators with measurement validity.[57] Training extends to staff hired prior to 2011 as well, with roughly 500 staff receiving evaluation training in the first year after the policy's announcement.[58]

Assessment

Assessment at USAID is primarily seen as fitting into program design, as with several other systems reviewed for this study. However, because USAID policy tries to develop a link between evaluation and program design, there is a tacit connection between the two endeavors.

---

[55] Rajiv Shah, "Remarks by USAID Administrator Dr. Rajiv Shah at the Center for Global Development," Washington, D.C., January 19, 2011.

[56] USAID, 2011a, p. 2.

[57] Author interview with USAID officials, August 12, 2015.

[58] USAID, "USAID Evaluation Policy: Year One—First Annual Report and Plan for 2012 and 2013," Washington, D.C., February 2012a, p. 3.

Figure 3.4
USAID Program Cycle

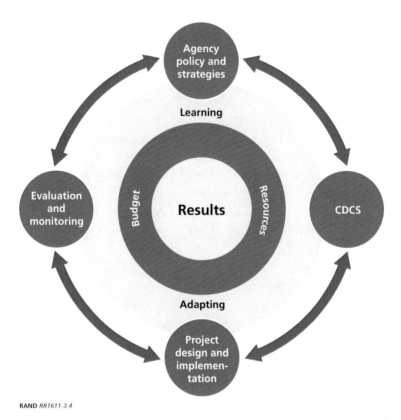

SOURCE: Adapted from USAID, "Program Cycle Overview," Washington, D.C., December 9, 2011b, p. 3.

The Country Development Cooperation Strategy (CDCS) is the guidance that drives objective-setting and the development of a logical framework for program design and evaluation. The development of the CDCS for a country takes between six and eight months and is the result of assessment-like consultations, as well as required assessments for gender and biodiversity.[59] However, assessments are also utilized in the project design process. These may be new assessments or

---

[59] USAID, 2011b, p. 7.

Table 3.4
USAID Evaluation Standards

Standard	Description
Integrate evaluation into design	Include evaluation specialists in strategy and project design teams, identify questions, plan for baseline data collection
Minimize bias	Disclosure of conflicts of interest, external evaluation experts as team leads
Ensure relevance to future decisions	Evaluation questions developed with stakeholders and are linked to future decisions
Use the best methods	Qualitative and quantitative measures that generate reproducible and high-quality evidence
Reinforce local capacity	Work with local expert evaluation leads, use host country systems, and build local capacity
Be transparent	Findings from evaluations are shared publicly and in a timely manner
Dedicate sufficient resources	Goal of approximately 3 percent of a USAID operating unit's total program funds to be set aside for external evaluations

SOURCE: Winston J. Allen, "USAID Evaluation Policy: One Year After," Washington, D.C., undated, p. 8.

repurposed ones from the CDCS process.[60] The assessments feed into the charter for the project, called a project appraisal document, which must be approved by the mission director at the operating unit and must have an M&E plan as a part of the project package. Beyond this, there are not strong guidelines for standardized USAID assessments processes.

Monitoring and Evaluation

As a part of the Department of State, USAID utilizes the existing Department of State MfR processes, including submitting data to a Performance Plan and Report. However, it is unclear whether USAID relies on this process to some extent or crafts a new process in which MfR is but a part. The logical framework created in the project design

---

[60] USAID, 2011b, p. 9.

phase notionally connects the CDCS objectives to performance indicators that can be monitored throughout the life of the project. Monitoring indicators may be taken from higher-level guidance as CDCS performance indicators, or they may be USAID standard indicators (which are a subset of Department of State standard indicators) or custom indicators.[61] In developing monitoring plans, staff are also required to disaggregate data by gender where possible. Downloadable templates that specify the frequency and method of data collection are available for download on USAID's website for performance management.[62]

Evaluation remains the pinnacle of the USAID AME process, and the agency provides training and full-time M&E staff to facilitate the development of high-quality evaluations. A key component of USAID's evaluation process is the integration of evaluation into the project at the outset, during the design phase. This includes a suggested Evaluation Scope of Work Checklist to ensure that adequate provisions have been made for independent and high-quality evaluations.[63] Also as part of facilitating the evaluation process, USAID guidance recommends that programs dedicate approximately 3 percent of program budgets to facilitate evaluation.[64] This does not include funding for routine monitoring. While these dedicated funds serve both to set aside money for external evaluation and to underscore the importance of evaluation to staff, removing the money from program budgets in immediate response to the 2011 Evaluation Policy created some ill will at the operating unit level.[65]

There is no restriction on the type of evaluation that units must do for a particular project, both performance and impact evaluations are conducted, and a variety of methods are used. Only innovative or large projects must be given impact evaluations if feasible, though the

---

[61]   USAID, "M&E Plan Monitoring Component," undated(c).

[62]   Available at USAID, "Learning Lab," undated(b).

[63]   USAID, "Checklist for Reviewing Scopes of Work for Performance Evaluations," undated(a).

[64]   USAID, "ADS Chapter 203: Assessing and Learning," Washington, D.C., November 2, 2012b.

[65]   Author interview with USAID officials, August 12, 2015.

evaluations are encouraged where possible, and a certain percentage of each program budget must be evaluated. As specified in USAID's Automated Directives System (ADS), a large project is one "that equals or exceeds in dollar value the mean (average) project size for each Development Objective (DO) for the USAID Mission/Office."[66] In practice, however, only about 10 percent of all USAID evaluations are impact evaluations.[67] This is partly because impact evaluations are less well understood, partly because they can be vastly more expensive than performance evaluations, and partly because the decentralized nature of USAID makes enforcing rules about impact evaluations more difficult.[68]

Relevance for DoD Security Cooperation AME

The AME system for USAID is very detailed and specific. While it has many interrelated processes, staff are trained in the process and provided with standardized monitoring templates and tools to facilitate the logical review of AME plans. This is directly relevant to the situation of DoD AME, in which templates to guide staff in how to think through evaluation design could be very useful. The depth of training, however, highlights a challenge for DoD: With a far greater number of staff, training may be very difficult to implement in depth. The emphasis on integrating AME into program design and the program cycle is also a helpful guidepost for DoD.

It is interesting to note that even in such a rigorously developed system there remains a challenge in conducting impact evaluations. This would surely be the case for DoD as well, in part because testing the logical assumptions underlying the development of security cooperation activities would be a challenge, even if the skill to do so were there.

Finally, at least in part, USAID has made strides in its evaluation policy and program cycle because of a strong commitment on the part of agency leadership not only to results-based management, but to a

---

[66] USAID, 2012b, p. 8.

[67] Author interview with USAID officials, August 12, 2015.

[68] Author interview with USAID officials, August 12, 2015.

higher level of rigor for AME.[69] Changing course, not only program-matically but also culturally, within DoD will require a similar, if not greater, commitment to a culture of evidence-based AME.

The Millennium Challenge Corporation Incorporates Partner Interests and Goals

Introduction and AME System

Founded on principles of transparency, competition, and beneficiary-led solutions, the Millennium Challenge Corporation (MCC) is an innovative U.S. federal agency working to reduce global poverty. The distinguishing characteristic of MCC's operating model and its AME system is its focus on the compact as a mechanism for structuring aid delivery. MCC uses the country as the primary unit of analysis, and each programmatic implementation is structured as a long-term compact with a partner nation. Because of this, the terms of the compact are well specified, including the terms for AME.

Assessment

For MCC, assessment is typically not labeled as such. Rather, the text of the compact reads like a summary of the extensive assessment work undertaken mostly by the beneficiary nation in order to arrive at the terms of the compact. Three documents form the foundation of assessment for MCC. The most important, from the standpoint of MCC, is the economic rate of return (ERR), a spreadsheet that estimates the impact of a proposed program on poverty alleviation.[70] In order to provide the ERR, MCC undertakes detailed collection of baseline data and provides economic projections with and without the proposed interventions. The ERR represents a "micro-economic growth analy-sis," focusing on net income gained and value added to the economy as the result of the proposed project.[71] A second document, the benefi-ciary analysis, extends the work of the ERR to include estimated social impacts on selected populations, such as the poor, children, women,

---

[69] Author interview with USAID officials, August 12, 2015.

[70] See, for example, MCC, "Nicaragua: Transportation," May 26, 2005.

[71] MCC, "Economic Rates of Return," undated(b).

and others. The guidance for the beneficiary analysis process is currently under review, and sample documents were not available for this analysis.[72]

A final document in the assessment series, the constraints analysis, appears to parallel the proposed country core assessment for security cooperation activities more closely. Unlike the other two documents, this report is prepared by the potential beneficiary government, with the support of the United States. Utilizing a decision tree methodology called a growth diagnostic, pioneered by Ricardo Hausmann, Dani Rodrik, and Andrès Velasco, the constraints analysis seeks to identify a few root causes of lack of growth in a country.[73] This document is used to guide program design. One benefit of the constraints analysis is that because it is written by the beneficiary nation, in principle it ensures that country's buy-in.

Monitoring and Evaluation

MCC has a detailed policy on M&E. It defines monitoring as "the continuous, systematic collection of data on specified indicators to provide indications of progress toward objectives and the achievement of intermediate results along the way."[74] The compact process requires that an M&E plan be developed soon after the signing of the compact itself. The M&E plan must specify a collection plan for several categories of indicators:

- Process Indicators: These indicators measure progress toward the completion of Project Activities. They are a precondition for the achievement of Output Indicators and a means to ascertain that the work plan is proceeding on time.

---

[72] MCC, "Beneficiary Analysis," undated(a).

[73] Ricardo Hausmann, Dani Rodrik, and Andrès Velasco, "Growth Diagnostics," in Narcís Serra and Joseph E. Stiglitz, eds., *The Washington Consensus Reconsidered: Towards a New Global Governance*, Oxford, UK: OUP Oxford, 2008.

[74] MCC, *Policy for Monitoring and Evaluation of Compacts and Threshold Programs*, Washington, D.C., May 1, 2012, p. 4.

- Output Indicators: These indicators directly measure Project Activities. They describe and quantify the goods and services produced directly by the implementation of an Activity.
- Outcome Indicators: These indicators measure the intermediate effects of an Activity or set of Activities and are directly related through the Program Logic to the output indicators.
- Goal Indicators: These indicators measure the economic growth and poverty reduction that occur during or after implementation of the program. For MCC Compacts, goal indicators will typically be a direct measure of local income.[75]

As with other systems, at MCC the principal focus is on the evaluation process, which it defines as "the objective, systematic assessment of a program's design, implementation and results."[76] Evaluation at MCC can include midcourse evaluation, self-evaluation, and final independent evaluation. For each compact, final independent evaluation is a required step. For the independent evaluations, conducted by competitively selected evaluators, MCC may conduct either impact or program evaluations.[77]

Relevance for DoD Security Cooperation AME

MCC has a mature and well-specified AME system. AME are not merely bolted on to project development and execution; they are integral parts of the program cycle. One aspect of MCC's work makes the overall task of AME easier: All programs are designed toward one result—poverty alleviation.[78] To begin with, poverty alleviation is more easily measurable than some goals, meaning that evaluations can be more quantitative and conclusive. This, in turn, makes it easier to structure impact evaluations than when objectives are more dispa-

---

[75] MCC, 2012, p. 7.

[76] MCC, 2012, p. 4.

[77] MCC, "MCC Independent Evaluations," undated(c).

[78] Author interview with MCC officials, March 24, 2016.

rate or less quantifiable, so it becomes easier to question underlying assumptions. In contrast, security cooperation has wide-ranging and difficult-to-measure goals, which means that a highly technical and quantitative AME system may not transfer as well to the security cooperation context.

Of course, MCC's AME system is not without its own weak points. As with security cooperation, MCC's poverty alleviation goals only tell a portion of the story. In fact, as with security cooperation, there are often unspoken, diffuse political objectives. While MCC is open about the fact that factors other than efficacy of poverty alleviation may come into play when funding decisions are made, documenting the logic of those cases remains a challenge.[79] Finally, if political will can trump technical considerations on the U.S. side of the equation, it is logically possible that the same could be true on the beneficiary nation side as well. That is to say that the logic underpinning the initial constraints analysis may represent not only technical analysis, but also political will. In one sense, this is positive—MCC should seek to work on the areas that the beneficiary nation is genuinely enthusiastic about working on—however, if those areas do not accurately represent the constraints on growth, then the larger economic impacts of the compact may not be realized. Overall, the deep involvement of the beneficiary nation in the development of the assessment and the terms of the compact provides a good lesson for members of the security cooperation community that active participation of the partner nation in assessing needs and developing the terms of cooperation can yield good results.

The World Bank Group Manages a Complex and Distributed Set of Programs
Introduction and AME System
The World Bank Group (WBG) is a large and distributed bureaucracy, conducting complex operations around the world. Its primary evaluative arm is the Independent Evaluation Group (IEG). It is important to note that the IEG does not sit underneath the World Bank,

---

[79] Author interview with MCC officials, March 24, 2016.

International Finance Corporation, or Multilateral Investment Guarantee Agency, but instead reports directly to the board of directors of its parent organization, the WBG. The IEG has a budget, which is separately approved by the board, that derives primarily from contributions made by the three component organizations of the WBG. In FY 2016, that total amounted to 1.3 percent of the WBG's total budget, or about $35.9 million.[80] This mechanism for organization and funding is designed to provide independence in the evaluation process. While it does appear to do this, and to create a hub for specialized evaluation expertise, the overwhelming size of the WBG means that it faces a challenge similar to that of other organizations profiled here: One organization cannot provide complete AME for all projects, countries, and sectors in its purview. In contrast with the AME systems of other organizations, IEG manages this issue through a sharp focus on evaluation, rather than providing assessment and monitoring functions throughout WBG projects.

Assessment and Monitoring

The World Bank's IEG focuses almost exclusively on evaluation, and assessment and monitoring are left to the operating units. Assessment appears to be considered a building block of the project approval process for the World Bank, rather than a piece of the AME system. For a project to receive funding, a Project Information Document is filed; in some cases this document, which provides several pages of justification for the project, may be the only publicly available "assessment-like" document associated with the project. In other cases, there may be a slew of assessments associated with the project, including social assessments of vulnerable populations and environmental assessments.[81] This is in addition to larger sectoral and country-level assessments that may form the underlying rationale for projects. As with DoD security cooperation programming, explaining the rationale for the project in the

---

[80] Independent Evaluation Group, "Work Program and Budget (FY16) and Indicative Plan (FY17–18)," Washington, D.C.: World Bank Group, May 14, 2015, p. 25.

[81] See, for example, documents associated with the recently approved project "Southern Agricultural Growth Corridor of Tanzania Investment Project" (World Bank, 2016).

context of the World Bank's larger country strategy is a key component of project justification.

Because the World Bank works across countries, sectors, and themes, a project-specific assessment may not always be the most relevant assessment tool. Beginning in 2014, the World Bank shifted to a Systematic Country Diagnostic (SCD), which, while not specifically called an assessment, functions as a master, country-level assessment that can guide both the country strategy and the projects undertaken across sectors and themes within a country:

> The SCD is a diagnostic exercise conducted by the WBG in close consultation with national authorities, the private sector, civil society and other stakeholders. It presents a systematic assessment of the constraints a country has to address and the opportunities it can embrace to accelerate progress toward the goals of ending extreme poverty and promoting shared prosperity in a sustainable way. . . . The SCD presents the best possible analysis based upon available evidence.[82]

The World Bank began implementing the SCD in July 2014, and as of January 2016, it had begun SCDs for 52 countries, of which 41 had reached the final draft and review stage, and 28 were considered completed and publicly available.[83] While there is not a regular review schedule indicated for SCDs, the length of time required to produce a final document indicates that these assessments are designed to serve as guiding documents for a significant period of time.

The terminology around both assessment and monitoring at the World Bank is confusing. There appears to be no single widely accepted definition of either assessment or monitoring. To the extent that the IEG does discuss assessment and monitoring, it appears to class these activities under evaluation, though not under a category of evaluation conducted by IEG. For example, in a 2015 report on managing evalu-

---

[82] World Bank Group, *World Bank Group Directive: Country Engagement*, Washington, D.C., July 1, 2014.

[83] World Bank Group, "The World Bank Group's Systematic Country Diagnostic: Online Consultation, March–April 2016," Washington, D.C., undated, p. 8.

ations intended to build evaluation capacity across the WBG, the IEG notes two types of evaluation: formative evaluations and summative or ex post evaluations.[84]

Evaluation

The WBG conducts evaluations at a variety of levels and in a variety of ways. While the IEG is the hub for independent evaluation within the group, it conducts only a fraction of all evaluation associated with World Bank projects. Typically, projects of the WBG are first evaluated by the operational units conducting the project. These are called self-evaluations, and roughly 270 new projects per year are evaluated in this manner.[85] Self-evaluation occurs in a variety of ways at the WBG with a variety of mandatory reporting requirements.

The IEG reviews this self-reporting using what it describes as a "rapid review" designed to evaluate the project against its self-stated objectives.[86]

Relevance for DoD Security Cooperation AME

The WBG succeeds in managing a massive AME burden through a combination of downward delegation of evaluation tasks and independent evaluation management. The downside of this is that most projects will be evaluated for how well they adhere to industry best practices, but the assumptions underlying those best practices will not be checked. This is mitigated by the conduct of impact evaluations by IEG. As with MCC, the World Bank's ability to conduct true impact evaluations using a control group is difficult to transfer to the security cooperation context. However, as a guidepost for DoD, this multilevel strategy of decentralized self-evaluations reviewed by an independent

---

[84]   Arianne Wessel, Nidhi Khattri, and Dawn Roberts, "Managing Evaluations: A How-To Guide for Managers and Commissioners of Evaluation," Washington, D.C.: World Bank Group, 2015, p. 10.

[85]   Howard White, "Impact Evaluation: The Experience of the Independent Evaluation Group of the World Bank," Washington, D.C.: Independent Evaluation Group, World Bank Group, undated, p. 21.

[86]   White, undated, p. 21.

central authority may help to resolve some of the burden of work that would otherwise fall on independent evaluators in the DoD context.

The fact that the IEG remains independent of the rest of the WBG at every level, including independence in funding, is admirable, but this not likely to be replicable for DoD. In addition, the existence of such a specialized and, to some degree, isolated AME function means that terms are not well defined and understood outside of the IEG. This specialization may work in the context of evaluations designed to be presented to the board, but for DoD's different structures, in which strong subject-matter and evaluation skills will be necessary to evaluate programs against the diverse array of security cooperation goals, the model may not be transferrable.

Conclusion: Other AME Frameworks Provide Many Lessons for DoD

This chapter demonstrates some common characteristics of high-quality AME, such as transparency; independence; adequate funding; and clear roles, responsibilities, and processes. There are also numerous ways to establish and apply an AME system, as illustrated in this chapter.

Table 3.5 highlights several processes inside and outside DoD, which we analyzed for their relevance to developing a DoD-wide AME regime.

From the military, there are cautionary tales about the challenge of applying AME to a disparate set of activities. The 1206/2282 programs, though, demonstrate how a simple tool—the logical framework—can guide better-quality AME throughout the project life cycle. This further shows that concepts made popular in the world of international development may transfer well to the military AME context.

In reviewing civilian AME, two organizations stand out as having particularly transferrable systemic lessons: USAID and MCC. For USAID, the relevant cornerstone of the AME system is having clearly articulated roles and responsibilities to a detailed level, supported by staff training and templates for M&E design, where possible.

Table 3.5
AME Processes of Interest to DoD

Selected Processes	Relevance
Army and Air Force security cooperation AME focuses on assessment of common factors worldwide and has been difficult to implement	Highlights the potential of comparative analysis of capabilities and the challenge of implementing global ratings
1206/2282 programs are distinguished by their up-front focus on logic model and evaluation visit	A logic model could improve AME process, though the evaluation visit has potential to overly attribute effects to program intervention
DIB programs have patchy AME efforts; where they exist, the focus is on observable qualitative indicators	Highlights challenges of standardization and data collection
Department of State Performance Plan and Report establishes country-focused objectives supported by standard M&E indicators; implementation suffers from lack of training and poor incentives	Standard indicators would offer benefits for DoD but cannot replace tailored evaluation; training and incentivizing are important
USAID uses the Performance Plan and Report, but performance M&E processes are tailored to individual projects	Clear roles and guidance on M&E offer lessons, but staff training is key
World Bank IEG conducts rapid reviews of self-evaluations and provides a dedicated budget	Highlights the challenges of managing a large number of evaluations with a central organization, as well as the need to consider the financial implications of an evaluation system
MCC: The primary goal of poverty alleviation is measurable, which facilitates evaluations of impact; emphasis is on bilateral compact	MCC example shows one way to integrate partner input

The AME structure is tightly linked to the program cycle so that AME is designed into the projects from the beginning. In the case of MCC, AME design is similarly a part of the larger compact design to ensure host nation buy-in, particularly in the assessment phase. While MCC's emphasis on impact evaluations is probably not transferable to DoD because of the less-tangible nature of security cooperation goals, the structured nature of the AME system is helpful to note, overall.

In the end, while the nature of DoD security cooperation programs as decentralized, diverse, and intangible in many goals makes AME a challenge, the experiences of other organizations highlight several ways forward for developers of an AME system. Chief among these are considering funding mechanisms to ensure adequate AME budget, developing templates and other process tools to simplify the AME process, and considering some level of standardization of indicators for AME.

CHAPTER FOUR

Proposed DoD-Wide Security Cooperation AME Framework

In order to satisfy the requirements of PPD 23 and meet its own needs for greater accountability and improved decisionmaking, DoD must formulate a strategic plan for integrating its various AME initiatives in the security cooperation realm into a coherent framework that can accommodate differences in AME purposes and contexts. This chapter attempts to contribute to this goal by providing a general description of AME methods and the parameters within which they might be applied, integrated, and implemented by major DoD security cooperation organizations. It outlines a conceptual plan that accepts many of the AME best practices and lessons learned described in the previous chapter—including definitional and procedural clarity, specified roles and responsibilities, M&E templates, standardized indicators, streamlined reporting, dedicated funding, and independent evaluation—while also making use of existing plans and procedures in major security cooperation organizations, such as the CCMDs, to the extent possible and desirable. Also highlighted in this chapter is the collaborative nature of the proposed framework, with multiple inputs and change recommendations being offered by the client and by other major security cooperation stakeholders and AME SMEs via a RAND-hosted workshop, as well as through numerous in-person and email exchanges with members of the RAND study team.

This chapter is composed of five sections. The first section defines the major elements of the AME framework. The second section explains how AME could be better incorporated into security cooperation planning, resourcing, and implementation processes. The third section suggests how key AME roles and responsibilities might be assigned to major stakeholders, and the fourth section describes the components of a comprehensive performance management system and proposes a way of standardizing the documentation related to AME guidance and results. Finally, we describe a potential method for prioritizing AME efforts, understanding that resources are limited and should be applied where they are most needed.

Elements of the DoD-Wide AME Framework

As Chapter Three showed, various organizations at different levels within DoD are already conducting assessment, monitoring, and/or evaluation of the security cooperation activities for which they are responsible. However, they are often doing so in a disconnected way, without clear guidance on who should be doing what kinds of AME, how they should be conducting AME and distributing their results, and how their AME efforts should be prioritized and integrated into larger security cooperation processes. Figure 4.1 is an idealized depiction of a DoD-wide AME framework whose basic elements are connected with one another, along with the security cooperation planning, resourcing, and implementation processes they are designed to support. Framework elements include the following:

- three AME components:
  - evaluation of security cooperation effectiveness
  - monitoring of security cooperation performance
  - assessments of the security cooperation environment
- three AME focus areas:
  - functional lines of effort that are used to guide the planning and development of security cooperation activities
  - programs that are used to resource security cooperation activities
  - partner countries with which the United States engages in security cooperation

Figure 4.1
Basic Elements of an Integrated and Prioritized DoD-Wide AME Framework

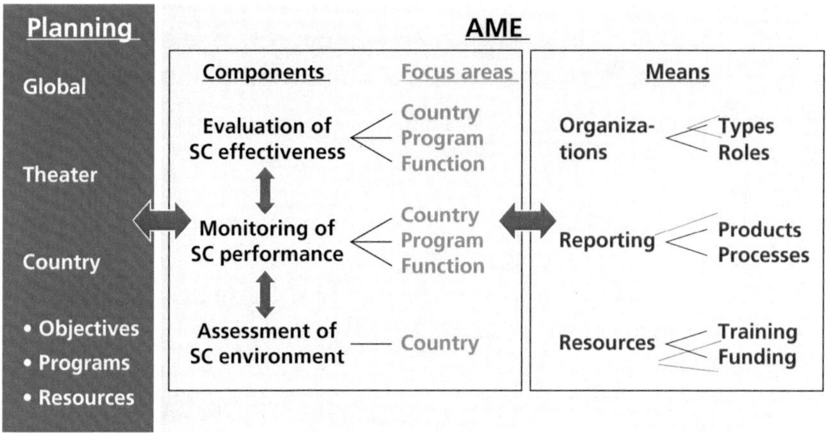

RAND *RR1611-4.1*

- three AME means:
  - AME roles and responsibilities of key security cooperation organizations
  - products and processes by which security cooperation information is reported
  - training and funding needed to perform AME in accordance with best practices.

The following subsections describe AME methods and their application, as well as AME focus areas. Subsequent sections explain how AME can be incorporated into larger security cooperation processes and the means by which security cooperation can improve AME performance.

Requirements of the Three AME Components Need to Be Clearly Outlined

Chapter One provided detailed definitions of AME derived from the management and social scientific literature and from doctrinal publications of organizations with well-developed AME processes, such as those employed by USAID and the World Bank. To align the three

AME components with DoD security cooperation efforts and distinguish them for managerial purposes, the study team developed (in consultation with OSD and other major security cooperation stakeholders) the following list, which spells out the kinds of information that designated security cooperation organizations could be responsible for collecting, analyzing, integrating, and/or reporting in each method category.

- An initial *assessment of the security cooperation environment* could
  - describe the planning objectives, authorities, programs, and organizations that pertain to the security cooperation activities being planned in a country or region
  - analyze relevant partner country military capabilities and political willingness to work with the United States, to include providing access to its territory and facilities
  - analyze the gap between current and desired conditions or outcomes
  - analyze political-military risks and benefits of carrying out the proposed security cooperation activity, as well as assumptions and external variables that might figure in the success or failure of security cooperation efforts
  - determine what can be achieved within the given time frame with the anticipated resources and establish planning milestones.
- *Continuous monitoring of security cooperation performance* could focus on
  - linkages among security cooperation planning objectives and activities currently being conducted
  - outputs produced, both intended and unintended
  - implementer-led monitoring of outcomes
  - collecting evidence to help determine whether desired results are occurring as expected
  - resources (personnel and funding) employed
  - planning milestones attained or missed
  - obstacles observed; risks identified
  - ideas for improving security cooperation programs and processes

- *Periodic independent evaluations of security cooperation effectiveness*
  could address
  - long-term outcomes of security cooperation activities, both
    intended and unintended
  - attainment or nonattainment of security cooperation planning
    objectives
  - cost-effectiveness of security cooperation activities
  - key factors affecting results of security cooperation activities
    (including nonprogrammatic factors)
  - adequacy of resources (personnel and funding), programs, and
    authorities in helping to achieve planned security cooperation
    objectives
  - appropriateness of planning and AME processes in helping to
    achieve planned security cooperation objectives
  - best practices in planning, resourcing, and implementing security cooperation activities.

AME Should Be Applied Differently at Different Levels of DoD

Table 4.1 indicates how AME could be applied at different levels
of DoD. Starting from the top, assessment of the security cooperation environment requires an in-depth analysis of local conditions—
especially the interplay among factors that might facilitate or hinder
the achievement of U.S. objectives in particular countries and regions.
Thus, the responsibility for this aspect of AME is best placed at the
operational and implementation levels, with the primary goal being
to establish an initial understanding of circumstances that could
potentially impact the status of security cooperation partnerships—
although such assessments could be aggregated at higher levels to
gain broader situational awareness or make programmatic or policy
recommendations. Ideally, these assessments would be conducted
using a combination of internal and external sources of regional,
functional, and operational expertise, depending on the partnership
under examination. Environmental (i.e., contextual) assessments are
the proper starting point to AME, but their utility extends throughout the process.

Table 4.1
Application of AME Methods

AME Method	Organizational Level	Goals	Organizational Type
Assessment of SC environment	Operational and implementation (aggregated at higher levels)	Initial understanding	Internal and External
Monitoring of SC performance	Implementation	• Tracking progress • Micro-learning	Internal
Evaluation of SC effectiveness (including lessons learned)	Institutional/policy and operational (aggregated at higher levels)	• Return on investment • Macro-learning	External

While guided and managed at higher levels, monitoring of security cooperation performance is the direct responsibility of implementing organizations. Its primary function is to provide the evidence of progress against a plan and to indicate whether things are on track. However, it also provides an opportunity to engage in *micro-learning*: that is, gathering and absorbing insights from the results of recent security cooperation activities that could be useful in improving the same or similar activities. Generally, monitoring is conducted with internal resources.

In contrast, evaluations of security cooperation effectiveness are optimally conducted at the operational or institutional/policy level and aggregated for higher-level decisionmaking. Such evaluations have wider and more significant purposes than monitoring activities—i.e., helping to determine the return on investment of security cooperation programs and country/regional LOEs as well as *macro-learning*— lessons learned from a systematic analysis of security cooperation activities over a period of time that might be applied to future operations. To better ensure objectivity and quality, effectiveness evaluations are optimally carried out by independent organizations, including specialists in evaluation techniques, which are not responsible for managing the implementation of the security cooperation activities or programs being examined. Generally, evaluations have a long-term focus: two, three, or more years.

DoD Should Focus Its AME Efforts on Countries, Programs, and Functions

Given the extent and variety of its security cooperation efforts, DoD cannot place all of its AME attention on a single unit of analysis, such as a project or program carried out by one organization that serves a particular functional purpose in a particular part of the world. DoD security cooperation activities involve dozens of different programs, are combined in multiple functional LOEs, take place in more than 100 countries, and are executed by many organizations in the U.S. military. To effectively plan, resource, and implement these activities, AME must be targeted on three related yet distinct focus areas:

- *Country:* activities conducted with a particular foreign partner (e.g., Australia, NATO)
- *Program:* activities funded by a managed set of security cooperation resources (e.g., the Military Personnel Exchange Program)
- *Function:* activities developed to achieve a particular operational or strategic end (e.g., building partner capacity for counterterrorism).

Although probably not a primary focus area for DoD, the *domain* could be a useful realm for assessing certain aspects of security cooperation, including partner capabilities that pertain to a particular operational dimension (e.g., land, air/space/cyber, or maritime). These supporting assessments could contribute service-specific knowledge and perspectives to more comprehensive country or functional assessments.

Incorporating AME into Larger Security Cooperation Processes

A key takeaway from our analysis of AME in DoD and non-DoD organizations, as described in the previous chapter, is the need to incorporate AME into overall security cooperation planning, resourcing, and implementation processes. If done well, this integration should enable major security cooperation stakeholders to

- determine progress toward military objectives, including the development of full-spectrum partner nation military capabilities
- test the existing theory of change linking the cluster of security cooperation activities selected to fulfill each objective
- ensure that security cooperation activities are progressing as planned and course corrections are being made when needed
- recognize and address the consequences of unintended outcomes.

This section describes a five-step cycle for integrating AME into larger security cooperation processes (see Figure 4.2). The cycle begins with an initial environmental assessment and collection of baseline data. It is followed by the incorporation of AME results into planning (step two) and program design (step three). Step four focuses on monitoring the plan and program implementation and taking necessary steps to adapt to improve performance, and step five focuses on centralized evaluation. In our description of the AME cycle, we have chosen to use the country plan as our primary unit of analysis. This is because country plans and country-level objectives (CLOs) provide a holistic perspective of the desired outcomes and impact of security cooperation efforts. However, the methodology and standards that we describe for integrating AME into country planning are mostly adaptable to the other two security cooperation focus areas: programs and functions.

Step 1: Conduct an Initial Assessment
Initial assessments inform CCMD theater- and country-level plans and support initial security cooperation program design. The baseline information collected through this process provides an understanding of the context, conditions, and capabilities immediately prior to the application of security cooperation plans, programs, and activities anticipated in support of U.S. government and partner nation objectives. Initial assessments describe partner nation willingness and propensity to implement and sustain assistance, improve institutional

Figure 4.2
AME Cycle

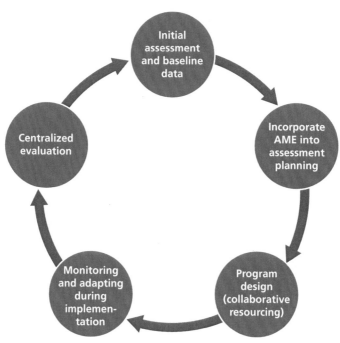

RAND *RR1611-4.2*

capacity, and build capabilities in the context of country or other relevant objectives and identify requirements, gaps, and risks. A focus on the DOTMLPF-P[1] framework provides a path for considering the full spectrum of relevant capabilities when planning for security cooperation objectives geared toward building partner capacity. Reaching more indirect goals of improving access with partners or leveraging partner support to address shared security concerns may require additional analysis.

---

[1]   DOTMLPF-P (which stands for doctrine, organization, training, materiel, leadership and education, personnel, facilities, and policy) is an acronym used in DoD's capability development process. It provides a conceptual framework for envisioning potential capabilities-based solutions.

Country-level analysis is the basis for all initial security cooperation assessments. DoD elements conducting initial assessments should ensure that ample time is given to desk study, interviews, and other preparation prior to sending individuals or teams in country to conduct more in-depth analysis. Assessments may be conducted without travel on occasion, when conditions require it. The desk study portion of initial assessments should be conducted by collaborative groups of CCMD SMEs with the help of outside experts, as needed. At that point, teams should be sent to the country to confirm the validity and feasibility of the preliminary plan and add depth and detail to the assessment, preferably in coordination with the partner. Country assessments should be updated periodically as a changing political or security context warrants and in support of monitoring efforts.

Department elements conducting initial programmatic or functional assessments should build on existing DoD and interagency country assessments. Circumstances may arise in which functional or programmatic assessments may precede a country assessment, such as taking into account countries on the latter end of a multiyear assessment cycle. Functional area assessments may be interagency in nature and should include representatives of the full range of expertise in the full-spectrum capability development framework. As follow-on assessments, functional and programmatic assessments could be undertaken to focus on those aspects of country assessments that pertain to gaps regarding particular objectives, capabilities, programmatic activities, or other concerns.

Step 2: Incorporate Initial Assessment Results into Security Cooperation Planning

Whereas initial assessment contributes programmatic constraints and risks that affect the likelihood of success, TCPs and associated country plans articulate theater and country objectives and describe geographic combatant commands' responsibilities for achieving them. TCP guidance and objectives provide an overarching framework for security cooperation country plans and activities, assess the partner nation's willingness and propensity to support DoD priorities, improve institutional capacity, and build partner operational and tactical capacity in the context of DoD's vision for the desired partner nation role. This process aligns closely with requirements planning and mission planning efforts and reinforces efforts to begin with the end in mind.

To obtain appropriate and credible data from the M&E processes, security cooperation planning proceeds as follows:

- *Incorporate the results of initial assessments into the plans.* A baseline understanding of the strategic and operational environments by multiple stakeholders and experts provides a clearer rationale for linking objectives to problem sets, which, in turn, reinforces the relevance of the logic linking the selection of a cluster of security cooperation activities in support of CLOs.
- *Develop SMART[2] country-level objectives to facilitate planning for desired outcomes.* This process helps ensure that the proposed packages of security cooperation programs and activities are together both necessary and sufficient for achieving CLOs.
- *Articulate a theory of change for each objective.*[3] A clear articulation of how a cluster of security cooperation activities and programs are believed to change or improve a situation in a country will help make the case for resources and other U.S. government and partner support, including in the out years, and help shape the M&E processes to follow.

---

[2]   Although the SMART acronym has been defined in a number of ways, RAND's recent report on objective development defines it as "specific, measurable, achievable, relevant and results-oriented, and time-bound." See McNerney et al., 2016.

[3]   A *theory of change* is a program description that explains how a series of early and intermediate accomplishments lead to longer-term results. A well-developed theory of change should also articulate the assumptions that underlie a program's existence and the process through which change will occur, and it should specify the ways in which the combined outputs and intermediate outcomes will lead to the long-term results.

- *Demonstrate the linkages, path, and logic (theory of change) between security cooperation activities, and anticipated outputs, outcome, and impact.*[4] Results frameworks[5] may be used to represent this path.
- *Adjust for level of resources and authorities* available at this stage.
- *Review and adjust the scope of desired outcomes* as needed at this stage and following program design.
- *Develop an M&E annex supporting each country plan.* This annex (brief narrative plus spreadsheet) provides a set of questions to help determine performance, relevance, accountability, and outcomes of the overall effort. At a minimum, it identifies
  - key questions to be answered by indicators[6]
  - baskets of three to five indicators each (strategic, capability, performance)[7]
  - targets, benchmarks, and milestones[8]

---

[4] *Output* is defined as the direct, tangible results of activities—i.e., a "deliverable" or product, good, or service directly resulting from an activity, such as the number of training events and the number of unit members trained. *Outcome* is defined as the desired result of a program or objective—i.e., a factor that describes the changes and results of activities within the described context, such as whether partner capacity is built to meet standards, to what extent, and within a desired time frame.

[5] A *results framework* is a top-down model that articulates the linkages between objectives and results expected from a particular strategy, plan, or program. It typically reflects the cause-and-effect relationships from inputs to outputs, to outcomes, and to objectives.

[6] *Indicator* is defined as a quantitative or qualitative factor that measures process (input), output, outcome, or impact in achieving an objective. According to one non-DoD M&E expert we consulted in April 2016, useful indicators are practical (not too expensive or difficult to get), reliable (when used repeatedly, you get the same result), objective (two people with different perspectives would agree that it measures the objective), valid (they measure what is important and closely tied to what we are trying to achieve), and direct.

[7] As noted in the introduction, performance indicators measure progress toward security sector objectives; strategic and capability indicators provide insight into contextual factors (political, military, social, economic) related to security sector assistance planning and programming—for example, the Government Performance and Results Act (GPRA) Modernization Act of 2010 and the OECD/DAC Handbook on Security Sector Reform.

[8] *Baseline* is defined as an initial set of data or observations of the conditions that serve as referents for comparison or control against which future changes, progress, or results will be measured—i.e., where we are today. *Target* is defined as a planned level of results to be achieved by specific dates, used to judge performance—i.e., where we want to end up. *Benchmark* is defined as the level of "best" experiences of other operating units, agencies, or

- anticipated data sources
- reporting requirements
- Offices of Primary Responsibility (OPR).

Ideally, the M&E annex should be developed at the same time as the rest of the country plan, with the understanding that additional expertise may be required to craft it and to identify appropriate benchmarks and milestones. Consideration of these requirements during an initial assessment process should greatly facilitate this process. The M&E annex also periodically validates or updates key findings from the initial assessment, including gaps, opportunities, risks, context, likelihood of achievability within given time frame, and resources.

Program owners and functional planners plan and measure different aspects of the same efforts captured in country plans. When developing or implementing programs in country, program owners regularly develop objectives that address the requirements outlined in global-, regional-, and country-level guidance, scoped to the relevant guidance that pertains to their programs. As such, they should seek to align their objectives with relevant CLOs when planning and measuring efforts at the country level. Program owners and functional planners should also incorporate SMART objectives, indicators, associated theory of change, and M&E specifications into their global, country, and regional planning.

Step 3: Incorporate AME into Mission Planning and Program Design
Mission planning and program design is a deliberate and iterative process that weaves together a diverse set of security cooperation tools and activities into clusters to achieve clear objectives. Translation of CLOs into a cohesive security cooperation program requires a clear articulation of what success looks like in the operating environment, as well as a cluster of indicators and associated metrics that illustrate whether progress is being achieved. Thus, this step of the AME cycle should be

---

partners who have achieved a high level of performance with similar types of programs. It enables comparison across similar efforts over time and space. A *milestone* is defined as ignificant steps or events identified for measuring movement toward achieving targets.

undertaken in a collaborative environment with the right expertise to ensure that security cooperation tools and activities are combined and synchronized to achieve maximum unity of effort.

Mission planning and program design for security cooperation focuses primarily on embedding M&E into country plans by applying security cooperation activities in a concerted manner to accomplish CLOs, in line with the theory of change and vision for success articulated in these plans. They allow security cooperation planners to spell out their assumptions regarding the linkages between activities, outputs, objectives, and goals at different levels.

The following are some best practices in mission planning and program design from our research on AME processes at DoD and non-DoD security sector assistance organizations, as described in Chapters Two and Three:

- Determine the package of security cooperation programs and other relevant activities needed to achieve the objective. SMART objectives help ensure that mission planning for security cooperation maintains a perspective on higher-order outcomes to be achieved, as well as on the strategic and broader U.S. assistance contexts.
- Recall that security cooperation tools and activities must be both necessary and sufficient to achieve objectives. Critical elements of a CLO that are inadequately addressed by security cooperation may require a rebalancing of anticipated outcomes, ways, and means.
- Weave together security cooperation tools and activities from multiple programs into LOAs or clusters of linked activity, forming a coherent, sustained approach to increase the likelihood that the security cooperation investments are absorbed, sustained, and effectively employed by the recipient. Ensure that full-spectrum capability planning informs the final product.
- With regard to each LOA, provide a brief explanation of how constituent activities are intended to interact to achieve the objectives identified in the plan, including a critical path (timeline and linkages) for reaching the indicators associated with the objectives.

- Populate the monitoring plan from the country-level M&E annex with the following information on key indicators and targets:
  - Measures of performance (MOPs) help determine progress relative to the accomplishment of tasks. MOPs serve primarily for tracking implementation and progress toward key milestones and targets.
  - MOEs—including strategic and capability outcomes—help analyze the attainment of desired outcomes for objectives and LOAs and assist with the analysis of second- and third-order effects.
  - Methods and tools will be used to collect measurement data and estimate relevant timelines, budget, and manpower needs.
  - Frequency of information collection (monthly, quarterly, annually)
  - Assignment of responsibility for collecting information (people or organizations)
  - Guidelines for how results will be communicated and used.
- Prepare for any needed decentralized evaluation by articulating the purpose of the anticipated evaluation and intended audience, listing evaluation questions and any additional information that will inform the analysis, and determining what information is needed, as well as where and how to obtain it and the timing and cost of data collection.

The mission planning and program design process outlined above can be adapted for security cooperation programs and applied to security cooperation–related functional LOEs in a TCP.

Step 4: Monitor and Adapt the Plan and Program

Monitoring the efficiency and effectiveness of security cooperation is a routine part of the security cooperation implementation process. Standardizing this process and linking it with goals and objectives identified during planning and program design is essential. Monitoring activities for security cooperation focuses on (1) activity or program performance, (2) challenges for implementation, (3) financial accountability, and (4) tracking whether desired results are occurring during implementation at each level. Monitoring is designed to maintain accountability and identify where course corrections may be needed. Monitoring activities should occur at every level, at all times. Responsibility for monitoring will vary according to the level, but all stakeholders (program managers, CCMDs, country teams) should be involved. Monitoring security cooperation augments and supports the CCMD's pre-existing assessment process by helping to determine whether stated objectives are being achieved or require modification.

Monitoring takes place at different levels and with respect to different focus areas. Individual security cooperation events should be monitored only to confirm whether the event was implemented, in the appropriate time frame, and to acceptable-level norms and standards. At the country level, the monitoring process includes a collective analysis of whether the ensemble of security cooperation activities is progressing in implementation and is demonstrating progress toward a clearly articulated objective, as defined by indicators for performance, strategic, and capability outcomes. Formal monitoring of plans and programs involves all relevant stakeholders and takes place at frequent, predetermined intervals throughout execution and when required by significant changes in the operational or strategic environment. Informal monitoring should take place continuously at the action officer level. The basic process includes

- review of MOPs to determine progress toward the accomplishment of tasks
- review of MOEs to analyze the attainment of desired outcomes and to assist with the analysis of second- and third-order effects
- review of changes in operational and strategic environment based on the initial assessment
- validation of or adjustments to plan execution or development of recommendations for higher guidance for modification of the ends, ways, or means.

Functional and programmatic security cooperation is monitored through a collective look at the relevant LOAs and programs. In the planning phase, LOAs and programs should be designed to identify what success looks like for the relevant capabilities being addressed during the given time frame, as well as what desired changes or outcomes will be. Planners should identify a basket of performance, capability, and strategic indicators to track progress and effectiveness over time. To assist in this process, DoD should develop a list of standard indicators organized into major security cooperation categories and subcategories, which could be functional, programmatic, geographic, or a combination of all three. Such a structure would allow for different forms and levels of aggregation. Organizing indicators into predetermined buckets would also help to ensure that planners without a great deal of training in M&E would select appropriate measures for their designated security cooperation activities.

Step 5: Conduct Evaluation at End or Midpoint of Implementation
Evaluations usually take place at the completion of a program or plan, but they may also take place at a specified midpoint in implementation or well after completion. Evaluations analyze progress toward key objectives or the sustainability of those objectives using indicators determined during planning or program design. This ensures a periodic complement to monitoring and the CCMD-conducted assessment process. Evaluations may look out over a longer time horizon. Also, the results of multiple evaluations capture broader lessons for future planning and programming processes and help to determine the effectiveness of major components of the security cooperation enterprise.

To ensure that evaluation is done properly, evaluation preparation is normally integrated into planning and program design and includes a plan for collecting baseline data and data over time for key indicators that demonstrate outcomes and impacts. Evaluations can be conducted midstream, at the end of an activity program or LOE, or ex post facto. Not all security cooperation endeavors require evaluation. Priority programs might include new or innovative pilot programs or global programs of a certain size. Priority countries could be those accorded substantial funding or a high degree of strategic importance. Monitoring data should be collected for a longer period after the end of programming for selected security cooperation activities to allow for the evaluation's better understanding of their long-term sustainability or impact.

Individuals or entities from outside the planning or implementation organization should ideally conduct evaluations. This both helps deal with manpower issues inherent in most organizations and contributes to objectivity. Centralized evaluations enable DoD entities to continue to assess and evaluate plans and programs for their own purposes, utilizing the new guidelines and process. Central oversight of evaluations and of process compliance is vital. Evaluations are highly recommended for country plans, functional evaluations, and regional and/or global program evaluations.

Assigning Roles and Responsibilities in a DoD-Wide AME Framework

Although the CCMDs have fairly well-developed functional evaluation processes, security cooperation AME in general suffers from a lack of structure and coordination, particularly at the program and country levels. Security cooperation programs conduct evaluations for the purposes of program design, but these can often duplicate previous work. At the country level, there is no consistent rule that determines how often a country is assessed. Monitoring data are often collected at the program, service, and CCMD levels, though they are often not labeled as monitoring data, which can lead this data collection to be confused with output-focused evaluation. As noted, CCMD AME tends to focus on evaluation. While evaluation frameworks can be quite detailed, as in the case of PACOM's evaluation framework, depicted in Chapter Two, they tend to focus predominantly on qualitative measures. Because CCMD evaluation is an in-house process, there is potential for biased results, and because there is little in the way of guidance or expectation-setting for security cooperation AME from OSD, evaluation frameworks focus primarily on answering implementers' questions, rather than those of policymakers. Also, tight and unpredictable budgets for evaluation mean that planning for evaluations is extremely difficult. Finally, there is currently no overall management and accountability structure for security cooperation AME, which would enable the reporting of data and analysis from various stakeholder organizations to OSD and the Joint Staff where they could support DoD and whole of government decisions regarding security sector assistance policies, programs, and resources.

Three Basic AME Management Options

There are three basic options for managing DoD's process of assessing, monitoring, and evaluating security cooperation:

1. a *centralized* AME model within OSD that would plan, oversee, and execute (or contract out) all evaluations, assessments, and monitoring functions.
2. a *decentralized* model, which is similar to the current model but employs OSD guidance, that would require DoD components and program manager to execute all AME functions based on specific policies, guidance, and templates (leaving space for some decentralized evaluation led by other parts of DoD, as needed)
3. a *hybrid* model, where the assessment and monitoring functions are executed by security cooperation stakeholders—guided by policy, training, technical assistance, guidance, tools, and templates—and the evaluation function is centralized in OSD to ensure independence and evaluations that are prioritized based on set criteria.

Each organizational arrangement has advantages and disadvantages. A centralized model would permit complete standardization, uniformity, and control of all three AME methods. This option would ensure that all security cooperation activities have performance management plans in place for centralized monitoring and for conducting evaluations. On the downside, the centralized option would require a very large staff of AME professionals, program managers, and new systems to cover all security cooperation activities throughout the enterprise, as assessment and monitoring functions would move from their current, mostly decentralized place. From a stakeholder perspective, this option would diminish learning and program management, absorb some AME functions already being performed by DoD components, and limit their ownership in this space. A centralized model may also be perceived as an inspector general/auditor role, as findings and recommendations from evaluations would be viewed within a compliance lens. Finally, no other U.S. foreign affairs agency uses this model. While it is employed by some of the smaller international donors, a centralized management structure makes it difficult to pursue a balanced approach to AME, as the more labor-intensive monitoring aspect tends to outweigh evaluation efforts.

A decentralized model is currently used by the Department of State and USAID with respect to their foreign assistance programs. If DoD were to adopt this approach, responsibility for all AME would rest with those closest to executing it, with an emphasis on learning, adapting, and performance/program management. However, this management option assumes a well-trained work force with specific training and expertise in AME, as well as robust systems to support all activities for policy oversight and compliance, which are not currently in place within DoD. Moreover, such an approach could produce uneven results, as it relies heavily on individuals, rather than policies, guidance, and systems. This model could also limit independence in what is evaluated and how the evaluation is conducted, as well as OSD's ability to ensure oversight and accountability of AME efforts. Finally, a decentralized model assumes that all activities are similar (e.g., development programs), which is not the case with security cooperation.

Employed by the MCC and the World Bank, among others, a hybrid AME model would provide security cooperation stakeholders with the tools and templates for using assessment and monitoring as performance/program management tools tied to their relevant plans, enabling them to use evidence and data to make programmatic decisions. In contrast, evaluation would be centralized, with dedicated personnel partnering with security cooperation stakeholders and SMEs to inform evaluation questions and ground-truth results. Such an approach could require OSD personnel to manage evaluation contracts and provide technical assistance to security cooperation stakeholders for assessment and monitoring. Funding, training, and technical assistance could also be made available for CCMDs to conduct decentralized, joint evaluations in accordance with policy guidance. One challenge is that this model relies on security stakeholders to be trained and supported in their monitoring and assessment activities so that a central unit can leverage their efforts during the conduct of its evaluations. Also, in the context of this model, evaluation may be perceived as an "audit" if security cooperation stakeholders are not used as partners. Consequently, specific and transparent criteria would be necessary to develop a DoD-wide evaluation plan.

Advantages of Hybrid Management Option

Under the hybrid model, the assessment and monitoring components of AME would be guided and coordinated from the top but decentralized in execution. As the bedrock of security cooperation activities, assessments establish the capabilities and needs of partner nations. Currently, however, assessments are conducted on an unpredictable schedule, often overburdening embassy country teams with visitors who ask very similar questions. To better manage this process, we suggest creating a country "core" assessment, assembled by CCMD staff with close coordination with SCOs, and including relevant insights from the intelligence community and the services where applicable. One model for this core assessment could be the ISSAF, a document developed to be consistent with PPD 23 guidance, and which draws on other best practice documents for defense sector assessment, such as RAND's Defense Sector Assessment Rating Tool.[9] While programs and services might still perform assessments for their own purposes, core assessments would be made broadly available and would be expected to form the context for these assessments to reduce duplication. To successfully implement a coordinated core assessment, a few additional costs would likely be required. First, the core assessments would require dedicated funds to support operations. This may be viewed as a reallocation of costs from other entities that would normally perform more assessment tasks. In addition, there would likely be a small cost associated with training CCMD staff to adequately perform high-quality assessments.

---

[9]   Agnes Gereben Schaefer, Lynn E. Davis, Ely Ratner, Molly Dunigan, Jeremiah Goulka, Heather Peterson, and K. Jack Riley, *Defense Sector Assessment Rating Tool*, in Agnes Gereben Schaefer, Lynn E. Davis, Ely Ratner, Molly Dunigan, Jeremiah Goulka, Heather Peterson, and K. Jack Riley, *Developing a Defense Sector Assessment Rating Tool*, Santa Monica, Calif.: RAND Corporation, TR-864-OSD, 2010.

Monitoring is a task appropriately conducted by implementers at each level of the system. In other words, program staff implementing security cooperation efforts should monitor their work, as should CCMD or service staff responsible for security cooperation activities. To some extent, this monitoring is currently being done through inputs into G-TSCMIS or through CCMD management systems, which track spending, attendance, and other metrics. In a hybrid AME framework, these monitoring responsibilities would be built on these processes but with emphasis on data collection on outputs and outcomes of security cooperation. Formalized training of personnel in security cooperation organizations would be needed but would likely entail small additional costs. In addition to this effort, the Defense Security Cooperation Agency (DSCA) and the CCMDs would need to play roles in the validation and integration of monitoring data, the former with respect to country and program performance and the latter with respect to CCMD-specific security cooperation activities. These roles would help to ensure that quality data are made available and structured in such a way as to foster good analysis. There would likely be moderate costs associated with the operation of these functions.

Utility of a Central Evaluation Organization
As discussed earlier, the challenges of security cooperation evaluation include the lack of a common definition of the term, absence of higher guidance on evaluation focus, in-house conduct of evaluations, and inadequate staffing for evaluations. To better manage this process, DoD could establish a centralized OSD evaluation organization to oversee the evaluation function. Additionally, this central office would empower security cooperation stakeholders responsible for assessment and monitoring functions by providing technical assistance; developing standards, guidance, tools, and templates; and assisting in developing training that focuses on performance management tied to plans. While CCMDs and other stakeholders would facilitate the hiring or development of qualified evaluators and provide supporting data and analysis to the process, this revised structure would support the key evaluation principles of transparency and independence, ensuring that evaluations are centrally stored, accessible, and separated from the

implementation process. Such an office would require funding and significant contractor support, given current billet limitations, as well as a permanent staff to perform the oversight function. In partnership with major security cooperation stakeholders, a central evaluation organization could enable DoD to plan and execute evaluations according to its highest strategic and programmatic priorities and comply with various standards and reporting requirements in PPD 23 and in draft legislation for congressionally directed reviews of foreign aid M&E policies.

Specific Organizational Responsibilities

In line with the hybrid management model described above, Table 4.2 proposes basic AME responsibilities for the major security cooperation organizations within DoD. These organizations include OSD; the Joint Staff; DSCA; the regional CCMDs; U.S. Embassy SCOs; service Headquarters and Regional Components; other defense agencies with security cooperation programs, such as the Defense Threat Reduction Agency and the Ballistic Missile Defense Agency; and the intelligence community. This proposal assumes the following:

- All major security cooperation stakeholders have an AME role.
- Roles may differ by AME method and focus area, as well as organizational level.
- OSD, the Joint Staff, and DSCA should have specific responsibilities for issuing AME-related guidance.
- One OPR should be designated for each AME method/focus area to oversee implementation and support higher-level decisionmaking.
- Provider organizations contribute aggregated data and analysis to OPR-approved products, as required by guidance.
- User organizations may further compile or exploit these products for decisionmaking.
- Any stakeholder could develop AME products for its use.

As Table 4.2 shows, we are proposing that OSD, the Joint Staff, DSCA, and the CCMDs collectively share the burden of overseeing and managing AME within the security cooperation realm. However,

Table 4.2
DoD-Wide AME Framework: Organizational Responsibilities

AME Organization	AME Method		
	Assessment of SC Environment	Monitoring of SC Performance	Evaluation of SC Effectiveness
OSD	• Guidance • Data and analysis user	• Guidance • Data and analysis user	• Guidance • OPR (country/program)
Joint Staff	• Data and analysis user	• Data and analysis user	• Guidance • OPR (function)
DSCA	• Data and analysis user	• OPR (country/program)	• Data and analysis provider
CCMDs	• OPR (country)	• Guidance • OPR (function)	• Data and analysis provider
SCOs	• Data and analysis provider	• Data and analysis provider	• Data and analysis provider
Service HQs	• Data and analysis user	• Data and analysis provider	• Data and analysis provider
Service components	• Data and analysis provider	• Data and analysis provider	• Data and analysis provider
Other defense agencies	• Data and analysis user	• Data and analysis provider	• Data and analysis provider
Intelligence community	• Data and analysis provider	• Data and analysis provider	• Data and analysis provider

NOTE: **Red** denotes lead security cooperation AME organizations; **black** indicates supporting organizations.

we are also suggesting that each of these organizations should have distinct roles with respect to AME methods and focus areas. OSD would be the principal purveyor of AME guidance and the OPR for the evaluation of security cooperation partner countries and programs. The Joint Staff would take on the OPR role for functional evaluations. The CCMDs would be the OPRs for country assessments and functional monitoring, whereas DSCA would be the office in charge of monitoring security cooperation activities at the program and country levels. Potential support organizations, providing data and analysis pertinent to security cooperation AME, include SCOs, service headquarters and components, other defense agencies, and the intelligence community. These organizations could carry out their own security AME activities, but they would not be required to do so.

Developing a Performance Management System

For AME to be useful for making enterprise-wide decisions, it must be part of a performance management system shared by all the major stakeholders. Based on the experience of other large and diverse organizations in the security and development arena, such as the Department of State and the World Bank, a security cooperation performance management system should have five principal components and one cross-system function:

- a *policy component* that details who should be doing what, when, and how with respect to security cooperation in general and AME in particular
- a *planning component* that includes an agreed-upon set of SMART security cooperation objectives, prioritized focus areas, and standardized indicators
- a *tracking component* that maintains an accurate record of past, current, and planned security cooperation activities, programs, funding, and personnel
- an *analytic component* that uses qualitative and quantitative means to transparently evaluate, aggregate, synthesize, and evaluate security cooperation results with respect to indicators and objectives
- a *reporting component* that communicates AME results to members of the security cooperation community at the strategic, operational, and tactical levels in a timely and consistent manner
- a *collaborative function* that permits major security cooperation stakeholders to participate in the development of the above components, comment on the results of the performance management system, and recommend ways to improve it.

Currently, DoD has developed or is developing some of the components of the performance management system outlined above. In general, however, existing components are neither standardized nor complete. Although several joint and service organizations have attempted to fill the void in security cooperation policy, their contributions have been inconsistent in terms of content, and their authority has been unclear without a definitive assignment of AME roles and responsibilities by OSD. TCPs include security cooperation objectives, whose progress is monitored and evaluated by the geographic CCMDs and the Joint Staff. Also, some programs, such as the Section 1206/2282 program, have structured planning and AME mechanisms. But there is no global security cooperation plan with a department-wide set of objectives, indicators, and definitions for priority countries, programs, and functions akin to the Department of State's and USAID's Performance Plan and Report process, Standardized Program Structure, and Standard Foreign Assistance Indicators. Additionally, CCMD country plans are uneven in their formulation of SMART objectives and milestones and related measures of effectiveness and performance.

OSD has envisioned G-TSCMIS as filling much of the performance management gap by providing visibility over activities and resource expenditures, linking activities to objectives, and contributing to AME. Although it has promise as a monitoring instrument, G-TSCMIS has not yet demonstrated a capability to portray the full scope of security cooperation activities and resources, in large part because those responsible for inputting the requisite data have lacked the incentive or ability to do so. Furthermore, G-TSCMIS will not replace the various performance management systems in use within the CCMDs and the services so long as it remains essentially an activity tracker that is not designed for operational- or strategic-level planning and evaluation. For example, country-level objectives, milestones, and indicators are not included in G-TSCMIS. Also, the system's evaluation component is focused on events (rather than countries, programs, or functions) and is generally considered unreliable because results are consistently positive and not verified by an outside party. While continuing to improve G-TSCMIS's ability to provide a common picture of security cooperation activities, DoD should consider developing another strategic-level tool for planning and evaluation that includes SMART objectives, the associated indicators to monitor progress against those objectives, and a limited set of indicators for prioritized focus areas, drawing on relevant data from G-TSCMIS and other sources.

Even without a comprehensive digital solution to the problem of security cooperation planning, tracking, and analysis, it is possible to envision a more coherent structure for conveying guidance from the top down and results from the bottom up. Table 4.3 shows how this might be done by incorporating AME information into existing DoD policy and planning documents, as well as creating a few new documents to cover certain holes in the AME process. In line with the AME roles discussed above, we are proposing that OSD take charge of setting general priorities for security cooperation AME in the Secretary of Defense's planning guidance, defining AME roles and responsibilities in a Department of Defense Instruction (DoDI), and presenting the results of priority country evaluations and program evaluations in a report to the President and Congress. OSD's Policy organization could take responsibility for overseeing country evaluation results, and OSD's Cost Assessment and Program Evaluation (CAPE) organization could take responsibility for overseeing program evaluation results. DoD planning guidance could direct that CCMDs and other components provide data for these reports. Most of this AME documentation could be published every three to five years. For its part, the Joint Staff would be responsible for providing a more detailed explanation of AME priorities in the Chairman's Planning Guidance, a compendium of best practices for security cooperation AME in a joint publication, and functional evaluation results in the Comprehensive Joint Assessment (CJA) every three to five years, as well as AME lessons learned via reports published by the Joint Center for Operational Analysis (JCOA) and the Joint Center for International Security Force Assistance (JCISFA), as requested by higher authorities.

Other organizations with proposed reporting responsibilities include DSCA, the geographic CCMDs, and the service headquarters. As Table 4.4 shows, security cooperation AME procedures could be described in DSCA's Security Assistance Management Manual (SAMM)

Table 4.3
Proposed Security Cooperation AME Guidance and Reporting Documents

AME OPR	Product	AME Content	Frequency
OSD	DoDI (new)	AME roles and responsibilities	Initially, 5-year review
	SecDef planning guidance	AME SC priorities (general)	3–5 years
	Report to Congress (new)	Priority Country Evaluation Results (OSD Policy); Program Evaluation Results (OSD CAPE)	3–5 years
Joint Staff	Chairman's Planning Guidance	AME SC priorities (detailed)	3–5 years
	Joint Publication	AME best practices	Initially, 5-year review
	CJA	Functional evaluation results	3–5 years
	JCOA/JCISFA reports	AME experimentation/ learning	As requested

Table 4.4
Additional Security Cooperation AME Guidance and Reporting Documents

AME OPR	Product	AME Content	Frequency
DSCA	SAMM	AME procedures	Initially, 5-year review
	Report to President and Congress	Global country/program monitoring results	1–2 years
CCMDs	TCP	Regional function monitoring results	Initially, 1–2 years
	CCP	Country assessment and monitoring results	Initially, 1–2 years
Service HQs	CSP	Service program monitoring results	1–2 years

and reviewed every five years. DSCA could also be responsible for summarizing the results of DoD's monitoring of security cooperation program and country-level activities in an annual or biennial report to the President and Congress. The geographic CCMDs would be required to present functional monitoring results and country-level assessment and monitoring results on an annual or biennial basis as part of their TCP and Country Campaign Plan processes. Finally, service headquarters would include results of monitoring the security cooperation programs they resource in their Campaign Support Plans (CSPs) every one to two years.

Prioritizing AME Efforts

Although monitoring is a process that is ideally performed continuously and comprehensively, most large organizations lack the resources and trained personnel to conduct in-depth assessments or formal evaluations of every program, country, or function on an annual basis. Thus, there is a need for security cooperation stakeholders to agree upon certain rules for prioritizing their assessment and evaluation efforts. This section presents some ideas for how this might be done.

Assessment Prioritization

Prioritization of security cooperation assessments could be performed by the central AME element to ensure that assessments are synchronized with other AME processes. Several factors should be incorporated into the prioritization process: overall priority of the country in U.S. strategy and guidance, the length of time since the last assessment, and the existence of any major changes in the security cooperation relationship since the last assessment. This last category could include any changes internal to the partner nation, such as presence of conflict or economic downturn, which would affect the partner nation's ability to engage in security cooperation activities. Table 4.5 shows a notional weighting for prioritization. In this framework, the country's strategic priority as determined in security cooperation and/or OSD planning guidance (row one) is typically the greatest factor in raising the prior-

Table 4.5
Notional Assessment Weighting and Scores

Measure	Source	Scale
Strategic priority in security cooperation and/or OSD planning guidance	Security cooperation and/or OSD planning guidance	5-point scale
Years since last assessment	CCMD determination	1 point per year
Change to OSD planning guidance priority since last assessment	OSD planning guidance	Binary: 0 or 1
Major changes to country security cooperation plan since last assessment	CCMD rating	Binary: 0 or 1
Onset or conclusion of conflict involving country since last assessment	CCMD determination	Binary: 0 or 1
Country entered/exited recession since last assessment	2 quarters of negative economic growth	Binary: 0 or 1
Other CCMD determination of need	CCMD determination	Binary: 0 or 1

NOTE: This table assigns a possible five points to each country for strategic priority, though no point system currently exists for this purpose. The prioritization scheme would require points to be assigned to each country consistent with security cooperation and/or OSD planning guidance.

ity of a country for assessment, with the exception of those cases in which it has been more than five years since the country's last assessment (row two). An additional five points are available to be allocated based on changes to the partner relationship, either from the partner or U.S. perspective (rows three, four, and five). This has the effect of giving equal weight in the prioritization scheme for strategic priority and rapid transformation.

In Table 4.6, we can see a series of mock rankings based on the three elements of prioritization: strategic priority, time since last assessment, and change to the partner relationship. The notional ranking highlights the interplay of these factors. For example, Country 4, though not a high strategic priority, ranks high on this list because of the length of time since assessment and the amount of change to the relationship since that assessment. Country 2 was recently assessed, but because it is a high strategic priority and the relationship is rapidly

Table 4.6
Notional Assessment Ranking

Country	Ranking
Country 1	5 + 3 + 4 = 12
Country 2	5 + 1 + 5 = 11
Country 3	4 + 4 + 3 = 11
Country 4	2 + 5 + 3 = 10
Country 5	3 + 4 + 3 = 10
Country 6	3 + 4 + 0 = 7
Country 7	3 + 1 + 3 = 7
Country 8	2 + 2 + 2 = 6
Country 9	5 + 0 + 0 = 5
Country 10	1 + 2 + 2 = 5
Country 11	2 + 1 + 0 = 3
Country N	1 + 1 + 0 = 2

changing, it is a very high priority for assessment. With such a prioritized list, the central AME element can scale the amount of assessment work to fit available funding.

Evaluation Prioritization

As with a more coordinated assessment process, a coordinated evaluation process would require OSD—in conjunction with other security cooperation stakeholders—to prioritize which security cooperation activities should be evaluated. Prioritization in this case serves to limit costs and facilitate better division of labor. In examining which factors are most relevant to evaluation priority, the RAND team selected overall country strategic priority (as determined in security cooperation and/or OSD planning guidance), priority of LOE (e.g., counterterrorism), importance of the project to the partner nation, cost of the project, and innovativeness of the project concept. This set of factors would allow OSD to focus on those projects that are strategically significant,

significant to the partner relationships, or higher risk from the standpoint of cost and innovation.

In Table 4.7, the strategic priority of the country and priority of the LOE form the largest portion of the weighting scheme. Partner prioritization, cost, and innovation together compose 30 percent of the rankings, though these weightings could be shifted, depending on senior leader preference.

In Table 4.8, it is possible to see how ratings for the various elements of the prioritization scheme, when weighted, affect overall prioritization. For example, Country 7, which is a high strategic priority but is otherwise a small project that is neither important to the partner nation nor innovative, ranks quite low on this list. However, in general, high strategic priority pulls countries to the top of the prioritization rankings.

Table 4.7
Notional Evaluation Weighting and Scores

Measure	Source	Scale	Weight
Security cooperation and/or OSD planning guidance	Security cooperation and/or OSD planning guidance	5-point scale	40%
Priority LOE	CCMD data or rating	5-point scale	30%
Importance of project to partner nation	CCMD rating	5-point scale	15%
Cost of project	G-TSCMIS planning data	$40 million or greater = 5 $30–39 million = 4 $20–29 million = 3 $10–19 million = 2 Less than $10 million = 1	10%
Innovativeness of concept	CCMD rating	Binary: 5 or 0	5%

NOTE: This table assigns a possible five points to each country for strategic priority, though no point system currently exists for this purpose. The prioritization scheme would require points to be assigned to each country consistent with security cooperation and/or OSD planning guidance.

Table 4.8
Notional Evaluation Ranking

Country	Weighted Ranking
Country 1	(5 x 0.40) + (3 x 0.30) + (4 x 0.15) + (3 x 0.10) + (0 x 0.05) = 3.8
Country 2	(3 x 0.40) + (3 x 0.30) + (5 x 0.15) + (4 x 0.10) + (5 x 0.05) = 3.5
Country 3	(2 x 0.40) + (5 x 0.30) + (4 x 0.15) + (3 x 0.10) + (5 x 0.05) = 3.45
Country 4	(3 x 0.40) + (4 x 0.30) + (4 x 0.15) + (1 x 0.10) + (5 x 0.05) = 3.35
Country 5	(4 x 0.40) + (2 x 0.30) + (5 x 0.15) + (3 x 0.10) + (0 x 0.05) = 3.25
Country 6	(1 x 0.40) + (3 x 0.30) + (5 x 0.15) + (3 x 0.10) + (5 x 0.05) = 2.6
Country 7	(5 x 0.40) + (1 x 0.30) + (1 x 0.15) + (1 x 0.10) + (0 x 0.05) = 2.55
Country 8	(1 x 0.40) + (1 x 0.30) + (3 x 0.15) + (5 x 0.10) + (5 x 0.05) = 1.9
Country N	(1 x 0.40) + (1 x 0.30) + (1 x 0.15) + (1 x 0.10) + (0 x 0.05) = 0.95

Conclusion

This chapter has attempted to provide a strategic, comprehensive, and integrated AME framework for DoD security cooperation that meets the requirements of PPD 23, builds on the experiences of other large security sector assistance organizations, and utilizes existing DoD policies, plans, and processes when appropriate. As described, the framework contains AME definitions and focus areas; an explanation of how AME should be incorporated into security cooperation planning, program design, and implementation; a proposal for assigning AME roles and responsibilities to major security cooperation stakeholders; guidelines for developing a security cooperation performance management system; and suggestions for prioritizing AME efforts.

This chapter makes several basic points about the application of AME methods to DoD security cooperation. First, while monitoring of security cooperation performance is primarily the responsibility of implementing organizations, evaluations of effectiveness are optimally conducted at the operational or institutional/policy level because of their importance for high-level decisionmaking. Furthermore, unlike smaller, less complex organizations, DoD must view the environment and the results of its activities from several different perspectives—in particular, country, program, and function. That said the country-level assessments—which describe a partner nation's willingness and propensity to build the capacity of their militaries, among other things—are the necessary first step of the AME cycle. Another crucial step is the development of country plans with SMART objectives, milestones, and measures of performance and effectiveness.

Security cooperation M&E—whether focused on a country, program, or function—entail a collective analysis of the progress achieved with respect to planning objectives, as defined by a small set of indicators, at least some of which should be standardized for strategic decisionmaking purposes. Whereas monitoring is a continuous activity, evaluations should be conducted on a periodic basis by those with sufficient expertise and independence.

A hybrid performance management model with decentralized assessment and monitoring and centralized evaluation would best ensure the quality and independence of evaluation results while permitting security cooperation organizations to continue performing many of their existing assessment and monitoring activities. For effective performance management, DoD will require automated tools to provide a common picture of security cooperation activities and to enable strategic-level planning and evaluation, as well as a coherent structure for conveying guidance from the top down and reporting results from the bottom up. Finally, a security cooperation performance management system must enable difficult choices. A set of rules can facilitate that process and provide transparency about prioritization rules for which countries, programs, and functions to prioritize for assessment and evaluation.

CHAPTER FIVE

Recommendations for Implementing an AME Framework

As discussed in Chapter One, the goal of this study was to help OSD design a DoD-wide AME regime for security cooperation. In this chapter, we highlight findings and recommendations derived from the analysis we undertook in our first three research tasks. In Task One, we analyzed the linkages among security cooperation objectives, activities, and resources at EUCOM and PACOM, highlighting their planning and AME processes and the challenges they face. In Task Two, we analyzed AME practices within DoD and beyond, evaluating their relative strengths and weaknesses. In Task Three, we described our proposed AME framework and analyzed the implications of its implementation. Although each task focused on particular organizations, the findings apply DoD-wide. Thus, we organized our findings and recommendations into two categories: (1) what is needed to support framework implementation and (2) good practices gleaned from existing AME efforts.

What Is Needed to Implement a DoD-Wide AME Framework?

This section highlights findings and recommendations from our development of a DoD-wide AME framework. The recommendations describe steps to translate the results of the framework into components of an effective AME regime.

Findings

1. We found that understanding of AME—including its elements, definitions, and how to incorporate it into security cooperation planning, program design, and implementation—varies widely across DoD. A small group of stakeholders appeared to have a deep and nuanced understanding of the concepts and were proactively designing their own AME systems as best they could within the constraints of DoD's existing organizations and processes. A much larger group was conversant with AME concepts and was undertaking limited but valuable AME efforts within their own organizations. Another group showed an awareness only of the basic concepts and lacked the motivation or incentives to take action beyond what was clearly and directly required by their leadership. Any DoD-wide effort at AME will require a common baseline understanding of concepts and guidance, using several reporting documents and supporting tools. While leveraging existing documents and tools is generally preferable, some new ones would be required to fill the guidance, reporting, and analysis gaps we found.

2. In testing the initial draft of our proposed AME framework with stakeholders, we found that no framework survives first contact with reality. The OSD-RAND workshop discussed in Chapter One highlighted significant implementation issues, as well as the importance of achieving stakeholder buy-in and obtaining feedback from AME experts inside and outside of DoD. Based on that feedback and follow-up discussions, we found that our revised framework and our proposed hybrid approach to AME oversight were generally supported, with the understanding that the details of implementation will require continuous testing and experimentation.

3. We found that because of DoD's size and the complexity of its missions, decentralized assessments and monitoring may be the best option. Assessments may be best at the CCMD level. Monitoring may be best at the implementation level, in close coordination with CCMDs and DSCA. Civilian oversight

requirements mean that evaluations may be best performed at the policy and institutional level. OSD's Policy component may be best positioned to manage country-level evaluations, while OSD's Cost Evaluation and Program Evaluation component may be best positioned to manage program-level evaluations.

4. We found that effective M&E requires a comprehensive and collaborative analysis of progress achieved against planning objectives, as defined by a small set of indicators. Developing effective objectives—ideally using the SMART construct discussed in Chapter Four—and collecting evidence against a manageable and relevant set of progress indicators is how planners lay the foundation for successful AME. While CCMDs and other components must tailor objectives and indicators in support of their own organization, a small number should be standardized for strategic decisionmaking purposes.

5. To minimize the need for new funding, a security cooperation performance management system would require rules for prioritizing countries, programs, and functions.

Recommendations

In light of these findings, we have several recommendations.

1. In order to help develop a common baseline understanding of AME within DoD, we recommend that OSD expedite issuance of security cooperation AME policy guidance, including establishment of roles and responsibilities. Guidance should come in several types of documents, such as planning guidance, program guidance, formal memos, and informal handbooks and standard operating procedures. Guidance should be supplemented with socialization at security cooperation annual workshops and other fora. The framework in this report can serve as a useful starting point for developing the necessary guidance and processes, but we would recommend at a minimum the following steps:

- ○ OSD should develop a DoD Instruction for AME that would clarify AME policy, terminology, roles and responsibilities, and standards across the defense enterprise.
- ○ OSD should institute a requirement for a report via which the Secretary of Defense and eventually Congress can share results of priority country evaluations and program evaluations.
- ○ OSD should chair an AME working group to determine the content, processes, and timing for AME inputs to the reporting requirements identified in our proposed AME framework in Chapter Four. The working group could also discuss how to better leverage existing tools like G-TSCMIS to support monitoring of activities and resources and their connection to SMART objectives—and a new tool for managing strategic-level planning and evaluation.

2. We recommend that OSD adopt our proposed AME framework and related hybrid approach to AME oversight. OSD will likely need to subject its AME guidance and other implementation measures to frequent testing and revising, particularly in the first few years. Over the longer term, OSD should strive to achieve a greater level of methodological rigor and transparency in its AME regime to improve AME performance, allow DoD to evaluate progress over time, and improve collaboration with security sector assistance partners across the U.S. government and internationally.

3. Regarding roles and responsibilities, we recommend that OSD work with the Joint Staff, DSCA, CCMDs, and other stakeholders to institute a hybrid performance management model with decentralized assessment and monitoring and centralized evaluation. As described in Chapter Four, this model would drive a system that delegates the bulk of AME data collection and analysis to CCMDs, military services, other defense agencies, and the intelligence community, while maintaining OSD and Joint Staff oversight of evaluation efforts. We also recommend that OSD and DSCA identify funding for a centralized

evaluation organization, as well as an organization to support and synchronize performance and effectiveness monitoring.

4. We recommend that OSD lead an effort to develop a template with a small, focused set of standardized SMART objectives and performance/effectiveness indicators to be used as a model. CCMDs and other stakeholders would supplement these standardized objectives and indicators with their own, tailored ones.

5. We recommend that the AME working group described above develop a prioritization scheme, using the notional examples in Chapter Four as a starting point.

Findings from Existing AME Practices

Our analysis of select DoD and non-DoD AME processes resulted in many findings, several of which are highlighted below. The subsequent recommendations are focused on concrete steps to apply the best practices that we identified at a DoD-wide level.

Findings

1. From an AME perspective, CCMD links among security cooperation planning objectives, activities, and resources are strongest when focusing on functions (LOEs and LOAs) within the CCMD. This is due, in part, to the robust approach that CCMDs take to analyzing their missions through the use of LOEs and LOAs in their TCPs, which are shaped by higher-level DoD planning guidance and reviewed by the Secretary of Defense. These links were weaker when focusing on program and country AME or when integrating security cooperation stakeholders outside the CCMD, such as military services and defense agencies. Although the Secretary of Defense has a role in reviewing TCPs, security cooperation planning (and thus AME) focuses on supporting CCMD leadership. CCMD engagement with policymakers is weaker in terms of AME reporting processes and sharing of lessons learned. In order for

the Secretary of Defense and senior staff to fulfill their civilian oversight responsibilities and coordinate with other Washington stakeholders, security cooperation planners need to be able to aggregate AME results, enabling OSD to provide analysis that cuts across regional boundaries.

2. The Army and Air Force have developed useful approaches to assessing partner capabilities. Rather than focusing on a particular desired piece of equipment or activity, they provide a more comprehensive analysis of existing capabilities and determine priority requirements to fill identified gaps. However, attempts at worldwide scoring of partner nations and efforts to incorporate service-level assessments into broader planning processes have been difficult to implement.

3. OSD's 1206/2282 program reported AME challenges, such as a lack of rigor in available data and mixed levels of support from stakeholders. Nevertheless, the program is exemplary for its procedural clarity, particularly its use of a handbook that describes its AME system in detail. The program's use of a logic model and the framing of evaluations determining progress toward one of a set of predetermined missions are also important AME best practices. However, the emphasis on an evaluation visit may lead to overattribution of effects to 1206/2282 efforts.

4. DIB programs, such as the MoDA program, often use needs assessments, execution plans, and evaluation plans in their AME frameworks, all which are best practices that could be applied to other DIB programs and beyond. However, the variety of DIB AME programs highlights the challenge of standardization and data collection for AME.

5. OECD has a noteworthy security sector reform handbook and a set of principles for evaluation. Security sector reform experts in the United States and internationally use OECD as a forum for discussing how to implement these principles and share best practices.

6. We found value in the Department of State's focus on collection of standard indicators for progress—a mix of monitoring and initial analysis—through the Performance Plan and Report.

However, implementation appeared to suffer from a lack of training and poor incentives.

7. We found that USAID, the Department of State, MCC, and the World Bank all use templates and standardized tools to make it easier for staffs to design their M&E efforts effectively and in ways that allow for aggregation of results to inform decisionmakers. In addition, USAID emphasizes training of all staff in AME.

8. We found that MCC's principles of transparency, competition, and partner-led solutions could provide innovative ways to challenge current DoD thinking about AME.

9. The World Bank's dedication of 1.3 percent of its total budget and USAID's recommended allocation of 3 percent of program funds to AME (mostly for evaluation) were important indications of the value these organizations placed on objective and sophisticated methods.

Recommendations

1. From a CCMD and planning perspective, we identified several related recommendations:
   - OSD should update planning guidance to direct the development of AME reporting in support of civilian oversight requirements, while allowing CCMDs and services to tailor some aspects of reporting for their own needs. The details for this reporting—including templates like those discussed in Chapters Three and Four—could be provided in the AME handbook recommended in Step 3 below.
   - Because best practices are not static, OSD should incorporate continuous learning concepts into security cooperation planning guidance.
   - OSD should adjust DoD security cooperation guidance and leverage planning and programming reviews to increase senior DoD leader focus on ensuring that they are getting useful reporting from CCMDs.

      ◦ OSD should sponsor a workshop session with a wide range of stakeholders on how DoD can better incorporate program- and country-focused AME into security cooperation planning and reporting. CCMD staff could discuss how they incorporate AME into their TCPs, while other stakeholders could discuss what data and analytic support they require to assess, monitor, and evaluate security cooperation. In addition to better leveraging TCPs, the workshop could consider the other reporting requirements discussed in Chapter Four.

2.   From a service perspective, we have two recommendations:

      ◦ OSD should incorporate service best practices in partner assessments into future security cooperation AME guidance.

      ◦ The Joint Staff should work with service security cooperation planners to develop an approach for injecting service partner country assessments into joint and interagency planning and programming.

3.   We recommend that OSD task DSCA to develop the following materials:

      ◦ a handbook for program-level AME, modeled on the 1206/2282 handbook but with additional materials drawn from the framework described in Chapter Four

      ◦ a set of logic models for common capability development areas, such as engagements, exercises, education, train and equip programs, and institution-building.

4.   We recommend that OSD include in its program-level AME handbook a section on DIB that incorporates best practices from the MoDA program and other DIB programs.

5.   OSD should engage with OECD security sector reform experts to discuss lessons from conducing AME in security sector environments and the refinement of its approach.

6.   We recommend that OSD build a menu of standard monitoring indicators, as well as a means for tailoring particular indicators to account for context.

7.   We recommend that OSD—using examples from the Department of State, USAID, MCC, and the World Bank—develop templates for staff to use in designing their monitoring and

evaluation approaches. This could help ensure consistent understanding of terminology, data requirements, analytic methods,
and timelines. OSD should also solicit help from USAID staff
in developing concrete steps to improve AME training within
DoD.

8. We recommend that OSD
    ◦ develop a personnel exchange between DoD and MCC staff
      to share best practices and stimulate innovation
    ◦ consider incorporating aspects of MCC's approach to pro-
      ducing an M&E plan developed jointly by the United
      States and the partner nation at the start of any program to
      strengthen host nation participation and will.

9. Finally, we recommend that OSD and DSCA meet with World
    Bank and USAID AME experts to discuss the processes by
    which different organizations fund AME efforts.

Conclusion

Various DoD components have made substantial progress in assessing,
monitoring, and evaluating security cooperation. Some CCMDs are
assessing partner capabilities with greater rigor, monitoring the outputs
of security cooperation investments and even monitoring outcomes
against functional LOEs in their TCPs. Some services are also improving their assessments of partner capabilities and monitoring outputs,
though CCMD and service efforts are not always aligned. And certain
DoD programs are utilizing at least some AME best practices. Contin-
ued interest by senior policymakers makes it likely that improvements
will continue. But without OSD leadership, these efforts will remain
ad hoc, and the results of improved AME will be almost impossible
to regularize and aggregate in a manner useful for national decisionmakers and regional/country planners working with security assistance
partners in other agencies.

By implementing steps like those recommended in this report,
OSD and other stakeholders will be better able to answer fundamental
questions about U.S. security cooperation efforts. For example, why is

the United States helping this country in this way? What's going on right now? What's working and what's not? Senior government officials and members of Congress frequently ask deceptively simple questions like these. As PPD 23 and Section 1202 of the National Defense Authorization Act make clear, however, simple answers supported by interesting anecdotes are not sufficient in light of growing budget constraints and a desire for greater oversight of taxpayer dollars.

Failure to create a DoD-wide AME system may result not only in noncompliance with White House and congressional mandates, but also in security cooperation planning with insufficiently rigorous underlying analysis. Well-designed plans may become a house of cards, undermined by poorly designed security cooperation activities, inconsistent application of best practices and continuous learning, poorly informed resourcing decisions, and failure to achieve strategic unity of effort. Incomplete or inconsistent AME may also impede the ability of senior officials to understand partner nation absorptive capacity, programmatic sustainability, and alignment of U.S. and partner interests.

Because improvements are already under way in various parts of DoD, the challenge is less about teaching concepts or building new systems and more about guiding and coordinating AME efforts, leveraging existing planning and reporting processes, and making security cooperation AME more valuable for policymakers. The findings and recommendations in this report, combined with our suggested DoD-wide AME framework, should help OSD provide the necessary leadership, primarily through more robust guidance, increased engagement inside and outside DoD, and a solid analytic framework.

References

Allen, Winston J., "USAID Evaluation Policy: One Year After," Washington, D.C., undated.

Author interview with Millennium Challenge Corporation officials, March 24, 2016.

Author interview with Department of State officials, August 14, 2015.

Author interview with USAID officials, August 12, 2015.

Chemonics International, "Interagency Security Sector Assessment Framework," Washington, D.C.: United States Agency for International Development, October 1, 2010.

DefenseAssistance.org, "Underlying Law for Defense Budget Aid Program: Authority to Build the Capacity of Foreign Security Forces," undated. As of August 23, 2016:
http://defenseassistance.org/programs/
law.php?name=Authority_to_Build_the_Capacity_of_Foreign_Security_Forces

Defense Institute of International Legal Studies, *DIILS FY2014 Report*, January 24, 2016a. As of July 20, 2016:
https://globalnetplatform.org/diils/diils-resources-for-public-news-stories/
diils-2014-annual-report

Defense Institute of International Legal Studies, *FY15 Annual Report*, February 2016b. As of February 29, 2016:
https://globalnetplatform.org/diils/diils-resources-for-public-news-stories/
fy15-annual-report

Defense Institute of Security Assistance Management, "The Management of Security Cooperation" (Green Book), August 2015. As of February 18, 2016:
http://www.disam.dsca.mil/pages/pubs/greenbook.aspx

Defense Security Cooperation Agency, "Ministry of Defense Advisors," undated(a). As of February 29, 2016:
http://www.dsca.mil/programs/ministry-defense-advisors

Defense Security Cooperation Agency, "Warsaw Initiative Funds (WIF)," undated(b).

Defense Security Cooperation Agency, *Fiscal Year 2013 Budget Estimates*, February 2012.

Defense Security Cooperation Agency, *Operation and Maintenance, Defense-Wide Fiscal Year (FY) 2016 Budget Estimates*, February 2015. As of February 26, 2016: http://comptroller.defense.gov/Portals/45/Documents/defbudget/fy2016/budget_justification/pdfs/01_Operation_and_Maintenance/O_M_VOL_1_PART_1/DSCA_PB16.pdf

Department of the Army, FM 5-0, *The Operations Process*, March 2010.

Deputy Assistant Secretary of Defense for Partnership Strategy and Stability Operations, "Performance Framework and Better Management of Resources Needed for the Ministry of Defense Advisors Program," memorandum for the Director, Joint and Southwest Asia Operations, Office of the DODIG, August 31, 2012.

Development Assistance Committee, "Principles for Evaluation of Development Assistance," Paris: Organisation for Economic Co-operation and Development, 1991. As of July 25, 2016: http://www.oecd.org/development/evaluation/2755284.pdf

DIILS—*see* Defense Institute of International Legal Studies.

DSCA—*see* Defense Security Cooperation Agency.

EUCOM—*see* U.S. European Command.

Government Performance and Results Act Modernization Act of 2010. As of April 11, 2016: https://www.gpo.gov/fdsys/pkg/BILLS-111hr2142enr/pdf/BILLS-111hr2142enr.pdf

GPRA Modernization Act of 2010—*see* Government Performance and Results Act Modernization Act of 2010.

Hanauer, Larry, Stuart E. Johnson, Christopher Springer, Chaoling Feng, Michael J. McNerney, Stephanie Pezard, and Shira Efron, *Evaluating the Impact of the Department of Defense Regional Centers for Security Studies*, Santa Monica, Calif.: RAND Corporation, RR-388-OSD, 2014. As of July 17, 2016: http://www.rand.org/pubs/research_reports/RR388.html

Hausmann, Ricardo, Dani Rodrik, and Andrès Velasco, "Growth Diagnostics," in Narcís Serra and Joseph E. Stiglitz, eds., *The Washington Consensus Reconsidered: Towards a New Global Governance*, Oxford, UK: OUP Oxford, 2008.

Independent Evaluation Group, "Work Program and Budget (FY16) and Indicative Plan (FY17–18)," Washington, D.C.: World Bank Group, May 14, 2015. As of July 26, 2016:
http://ieg.worldbankgroup.org/Data/fy16_ieg_wp_budget.pdf

Inspector General Report, "Defense Institution Reform Initiative Program Elements Need to Be Defined," 2012a. As of February 29, 2016:
http://www.dodig.mil/pubs/documents/DODIG-2013-019.pdf

Inspector General Report, "Performance Framework and Better Management of Resources Needed for the Ministry of Defense Advisors Program," Report No. DODIG-2013-005, October 23, 2012b. As of February 29, 2016:
http://www.dodig.mil/pubs/documents/DODIG-2013-005.pdf

Interviews with EUCOM headquarters officials, in-person interviews with author, February 10, 19, and 20; April 7 and 8; and May 12 and 13, 2015.

Joint Publication 5-0, *Joint Operational Planning*, Washington, D.C., August 11, 2011.

MCC—*see* Millennium Challenge Corporation.

McCarney, R., J. Warner, S. Iliffe, R. van Haselen, M. Griffin, and P. Fisher, "The Hawthorne Effect: A Randomised, Controlled Trial," *BMC Medical Research Methodology*, Vol. 7, No. 30, 2007.

McNerney, Michael J., Jefferson P. Marquis, S. Rebecca Zimmerman, and Ariel Klein, *SMART Security Cooperation Objectives: Improving DoD Planning and Guidance*, Santa Monica, Calif.: RAND Corporation, RR-1430-OSD, 2016. As of July 26, 2016:
http://www.rand.org/pubs/research_reports/RR1430.html

Millennium Challenge Corporation "Beneficiary Analysis," undated(a). As of March 31, 2016:
https://mcc.gov/our-impact/beneficiary-analysis

Millennium Challenge Corporation, "Economic Rates of Return," undated(b). As of March 31, 2016:
https://mcc.gov/our-impact/err

Millennium Challenge Corporation, "MCC Independent Evaluations," undated(c). As of April 1, 2016:
https://www.mcc.gov/resources/doc/factsheet-mccs-independent-evaluations

Millennium Challenge Corporation, "Nicaragua: Transportation," May 26, 2005. As of July 26, 2016:
https://assets.mcc.gov/documents/mcc-err-nicaragua-transportation.xls

Millennium Challenge Corporation, *Policy for Monitoring and Evaluation of Compacts and Threshold Programs*, Washington, D.C., May 1, 2012. As of July 25, 2016:
https://assets.mcc.gov/guidance/policy-050112-monitoring-and-evaluation.pdf

Moroney, Jennifer D. P., Beth Grill, Joe Hogler, Lianne Kennedy-Boudali, and Christopher Paul, *How Successful Are U.S. Efforts to Build Capacity in Developing Countries? A Framework to Assess the Global Train and Equip "1206" Program,* Santa Monica, Calif.: RAND Corporation, TR-1121-OSD, 2011. As of July 18, 2016:
http://www.rand.org/pubs/technical_reports/TR1121.html

Moroney, Jennifer D. P., Joe Hogler, Jefferson P. Marquis, Christopher Paul, John E. Peters, and Beth Grill, *Developing an Assessment Framework for U.S. Air Force Building Partnerships Programs,* Santa Monica, Calif.: RAND Corporation, MG-868-AF, 2010. As of July 18, 2016:
http://www.rand.org/pubs/monographs/MG868.html

Moroney, Jennifer D. P., Jefferson P. Marquis, Cathryn Quantic Thurston, and Gregory F. Treverton, *A Framework to Assess Programs for Building Partnerships,* Santa Monica, Calif.: RAND Corporation, MG-863-OSD, 2009. As of July 18, 2016:
http://www.rand.org/pubs/monographs/MG863.html

Moroney, Jennifer D. P., David E. Thaler, and Joe Hogler, *Review of Security Cooperation Mechanisms Combatant Commands Utilize to Build Partner Capacity,* Santa Monica, Calif.: RAND Corporation, RR-413-OSD, 2013. As of July 18, 2016:
http://www.rand.org/pubs/research_reports/RR413.html

Moroney, Jennifer D. P., Aidan Kirby Winn, Jeffrey Engstrom, Joe Hogler, Thomas-Durell Young, and Michelle Spencer, *Assessing the Effectiveness of the International Counterproliferation Program,* Santa Monica, Calif.: RAND Corporation, TR-981-DTRA, 2011. As of July 18, 2016:
http://www.rand.org/pubs/technical_reports/TR981.html

National Defense Authorization Act for Fiscal Year 2016 (S. 1356). As of September 13, 2016:
https://www.govtrack.us/congress/bills/114/s1356

Organisation for Economic Co-operation and Development, *OECD DAC Handbook on Security Sector Reform: Supporting Security and Justice,* February 25, 2008. As of July 17, 2016:
http://www.oecd.org/dac/governance-peace/conflictfragilityandresilience/
oecddachandbookonsecuritysystemreformsupportingsecurityandjustice.htm

Partnership for Peace Consortium, "Defense Education Enhancement Program," undated. As of February 29, 2016:
http://www.pfp-consortium.org/index.php/activities/
defense-education-enhancement-program-deep

Paul, Christopher, Brian J. Gordon, Jennifer D. P. Moroney, Lisa Saum-Manning, Beth Grill, Colin P. Clarke, and Heather Peterson, *A Building Partner Capacity Assessment Framework: Tracking Inputs, Outputs, Outcomes, Disrupters, and Workarounds*, Santa Monica, Calif.: RAND Corporation, RR-935-OSD, 2015. As of July 26, 2016:
http://www.rand.org/pubs/research_reports/RR935.html

Perry, Walter L., Stuart E. Johnson, Stephanie Pezard, Gillian S. Oak, David Stebbins, and Chaoling Feng, *Defense Institution Building: An Assessment*, Santa Monica, Calif.: RAND Corporation, RR-1176-OSD, 2016. As of July 26, 2016:
http://www.rand.org/pubs/research_reports/RR1176.html

Popovic, Nicola, *Security Sector Reform Assessment, Monitoring & Evaluation and Gender (Tool 11)*, Geneva Centre for the Democratic Control of Armed Forces (DCAF), 2008.

PPD 23—*see* White House Office of the Press Secretary.

RAND CCMD interviews conducted during FY 2014–FY 2015.

Ravinsky, Jeremy, "The Pentagon's Security Assistance Wasteland," *thehill.com*, November 11, 2015.

Schaefer, Agnes Gereben, Lynn E. Davis, Ely Ratner, Molly Dunigan, Jeremiah Goulka, Heather Peterson, and K. Jack Riley, *Defense Sector Assessment Rating Tool*, in Agnes Gereben Schaefer, Lynn E. Davis, Ely Ratner, Molly Dunigan, Jeremiah Goulka, Heather Peterson, and K. Jack Riley, *Developing a Defense Sector Assessment Rating Tool,* Santa Monica, Calif.: RAND Corporation, TR-864-OSD, 2010. As of July 26, 2016:
http://www.rand.org/pubs/technical_reports/TR864.html

Science Applications International Corporation, *The Assessment Process for Section 1206 Global Train and Equip Programs*, briefing, October 2013.

Shah, Rajiv, "Remarks by USAID Administrator Dr. Rajiv Shah at the Center for Global Development," Washington, D.C., January 19, 2011. As of July 26, 2016:
https://www.usaid.gov/news-information/speeches/
remarks-usaid-administrator-dr-rajiv-shah-center-global-development

Thaler, David E., Michael J. McNerney, Beth Grill, Jefferson P. Marquis, and Amanda Kadlec, *From Patchwork to Framework: A Review of Title 10 Authorities for Security Cooperation*, Santa Monica, Calif.: RAND Corporation, RR-1438-OSD, 2016. As of July 18, 2016:
http://www.rand.org/pubs/research_reports/RR1438.html

United States Mission to the United Nations, "UN Transparency and Accountability Initiative," undated. As of April 11, 2016:
http://usun.state.gov/about/2196/6657

USAID—*see* U.S. Agency for International Development.

U.S. Agency for International Development, "Checklist for Reviewing Scopes of Work for Performance Evaluations," undated(a). As of July 26, 2016:
http://pdf.usaid.gov/pdf_docs/pnadu534.pdf

U.S. Agency for International Development, "Learning Lab," undated(b). As of May 15, 2016:
https://usaidlearninglab.org

U.S. Agency for International Development, "M&E Plan Monitoring Component," undated(c). As of April 6, 2016:
http://usaidprojectstarter.org/content/me-plan-monitoring-component

U.S. Agency for International Development, "Project Baselines and Targets Template," undated(d). As of April 6, 2016:
http://usaidprojectstarter.org/content/project-baselines-and-targets-template

U.S. Agency for International Development, "Interagency Security Sector Assessment Framework," Washington, D.C., October 1, 2010. As of July 26, 2016:
http://pdf.usaid.gov/pdf_docs/PA00HWJX.pdf

U.S. Agency for International Development, "USAID Evaluation Policy," Washington, D.C., January 2011a. As of July 26, 2016:
http://www.usaid.gov/sites/default/files/documents/1868/USAIDEvaluationPolicy.pdf

U.S. Agency for International Development, "Program Cycle Overview," Washington, D.C., December 9, 2011b. As of July 26, 2016:
http://pdf.usaid.gov/pdf_docs/Pdacs774.pdf

U.S. Agency for International Development, "USAID Evaluation Policy: Year One—First Annual Report and Plan for 2012 and 2013," Washington, D.C., February 2012a. As of July 26, 2016:
https://usaidlearninglab.org/sites/default/files/resource/files/usaid_evaluation_policy_year_one.pdf

U.S. Agency for International Development, "ADS Chapter 203: Assessing and Learning," Washington, D.C., November 2, 2012b. As of July 26, 2016:
https://www.usaid.gov/sites/default/files/documents/1870/203.pdf

U.S. Agency for International Development, *Performance Management Plan (PMP) Toolkit, A Guide for Missions on Planning for, Developing, Updating, and Actively Using a PMP*, Washington, D.C., October 2013. As of April 11, 2016:
http://usaidprojectstarter.org/sites/default/files/resources/pdfs/PMP-Toolkit.pdf

U.S. Department of State, *Leading Through Civilian Power: The First Quadrennial Diplomacy and Development Review*, Washington, D.C., 2010, pp. 188–204. As of July 26, 2016:
http://www.state.gov/documents/organization/153142.pdf

U.S. Department of State, "Global Peace Operations Initiative (GPOI): Program Monitoring and Evaluation," Washington, D.C., August 29, 2011. As of July 26, 2016:
http://www.state.gov/t/pm/ppa/gpoi/c47010.htm

U.S. Department of State, "Department of State Evaluation Policy," Washington, D.C., January 29, 2015a. As of July 18, 2016:
http://www.state.gov/s/d/rm/rls/evaluation/2015/236970.htm

U.S. Department of State, "Evaluation of the Office of U.S. Foreign Assistance Resources' Implementation of the Managing for Results Framework," Washington, D.C., December 30, 2015b. As of July 18, 2016:
http://www.state.gov/documents/organization/251381.pdf

U.S. Department of State and U.S. Agency for International Development, *FY 2014 Annual Performance Report, FY 2016 Annual Performance Plan*, undated. As of August 23, 2016:
https://www.usaid.gov/sites/default/files/documents/1868/State-USAID_FY16_APP_FY%2014_APR.pdf

U.S. Department of State and U.S. Agency for International Development, *FY 2015 Joint Summary of Performance and Financial Information*, 2015.

U.S. European Command, "J5/8—Policy, Strategy, Partnering and Capabilities," undated. As of July 18, 2016:
http://www.eucom.mil/organization/command-structure/
j5-8-policy-strategy-partnering-and-capabilities

U.S. General Accounting Office, *Managing for Results: Agencies' Annual Performance Plans Can Help Address Strategic Planning Challenges*, Washington, D.C., January 1998. As of July 26, 2016:
http://oai.dtic.mil/oai/
oai?verb=getRecord&metadataPrefix=html&identifier=ADA337199

U.S. Government Accountability Office, *NATO Partnership: DoD Needs to Assess U.S. Assistance in Response to Changes in the Partnership for Peace Program*, Washington, D.C., GAO-10-1015, September 2010. As of February 29, 2016:
http://www.gao.gov/new.items/d101015.pdf

U.S. Government Accountability Office, *Combating Terrorism: State Department Can Improve Management of East Africa Program*, Washington, D.C., June 2014a. As of July 26, 2016:
http://www.gao.gov/assets/670/664126.pdf

U.S. Government Accountability Office, *Combating Terrorism: U.S. Efforts in Northwest Africa Would Be Strengthened by Enhanced Program Management*, Washington, D.C., June 2014b. As of July 26, 2016:
http://www.gao.gov/assets/670/664337.pdf

U.S. Government Accountability Office, *High-Risk Series: An Update*, Washington, D.C., GAO-15-290, February 2015.

Wade, D. T., "Goal Setting in Rehabilitation: An Overview of What, Why and How," *Clinical Rehabilitation*, Vol. 23, No. 4, April 1, 2009.

Wessel, Arianne, Nidhi Khattri, and Dawn Roberts, "Managing Evaluations: A How-To Guide For Managers and Commissioners of Evaluation," Washington, D.C.: World Bank Group, 2015. As of July 18, 2016:
https://ieg.worldbankgroup.org/Data/reports/ecd_man_evals.pdf

White, Howard, "Impact Evaluation: The Experience of the Independent Evaluation Group of the World Bank," Washington, D.C.: Independent Evaluation Group, World Bank Group, undated. As of July 18, 2016:
http://ieg.worldbank.org/Data/reports/impact_evaluation.pdf

White House Office of Management and Budget, Government Performance Results Act of 1993. As of April 11, 2016:
https://www.whitehouse.gov/omb/mgmt-gpra/gplaw2m

White House Office of the Press Secretary, *Fact Sheet: U.S. Security Sector Assistance Policy*, April 5, 2013. As of September 13, 2016:
https://www.whitehouse.gov/the-press-office/2013/04/05/fact-sheet-us-security-sector-assistance-policy

World Bank, "Southern Agricultural Growth Corridor of Tanzania Investment Project," 2016. As of July 19, 2016:
http://www.worldbank.org/projects/P125728/tanzania-southern-agriculture-growth-corridor-investment-project?lang=en&tab=overview

World Bank Group, "The World Bank Group's Systematic Country Diagnostic: Online Consultation, March–April 2016," Washington, D.C., undated. As of July 18, 2016:
https://consultations.worldbank.org/Data/hub/files/consultation-template/world-bank-groups-systematic-country-diagnostic-online-consultations/en/materials/scd_online_consultation-english.pdf

World Bank Group, *World Bank Group Directive: Country Engagement*, Washington, D.C., July 1, 2014. As of July 19, 2016:
http://siteresources.worldbank.org/EXTOPMANUAL/Resources/EntireOM_ExternalJuly28-2014.pdf

World Bank Independent Evaluation Group, *World Bank Group Impact Evaluations: Relevance and Effectiveness*, 2012.